THE *Rhys* TRADITION

THE *Rhys* TRADITION
Tracing the Reese Family Name

ROBERT L. JOHNSON

ROBERT L. JOHNSON
127 Churchill Ln
Niles, MI 49120-8999

THE RHYS TRADITION—Tracing the Reese Family Name
© 2005 by Robert L. Johnson
Library of Congress Control Number: 2005907714
Cover and book design by James W. Johnson
Castle photos © www.castlesofwales.org
All rights reserved
Printed in U.S.A.
ISBN 0-9779168-0-4

This treatise is dedicated to the memory of
those whose valiant efforts in the distant past,
and to those, who in recent times,
have contributed of their time and
talent to a study of the
Rhys (Reese) family

and

To the honor and dignity of our ancestors
in response to the Fifth Commandment
"Honor thy Father and thy Mother"
—Exodus 20:12. (KJV) (23).

"Hereditary honors are a noble and
splendid treasure to descendants."
—Greek philosopher, Plato
c 427–347 B.C.

WEOBLEY CASTLE
a Rhys castle near Gowerton, West Glamorgan, Wales (p. 117)

Contents

Acknowledgments . . . . *ix*
Preface . . . . *xiii*

PART I — INTRODUCTION

1. Chronology of Events 1
2. The Name: Rhys to Reese 7
3. A Coat of Arms 11

PART II — A HISTORICAL PERSPECTIVE

4. The Celts 17
5. The Britons 23
6. The Welsh 33
7. The Legendary King Arthur 43
8. The Wars of the Roses 47

PART III — THE WELSH CULTURE

9. The People 51
10. The Music 61
11. Christianity 73
12. Emigrants 97

PART IV — THE HISTORICAL RHYS

13 A Roots Research 101
14 The Castles in Rhys History 107
15 Sir Rhys ap Thomas 123
16 The Great Betrayal 137

PART V — A REES FAMILY IN AMERICA

17 A Dutch Connection 143
18 A French Connection 149
19 Pioneers—New Amsterdam Westward. 155
20 The Rees–Gillett Reunions 163

PART VI — A REES FAMILY IN MICHIGAN

21 The Pioneer Brothers 213
22 The Jacob Rees Family 221
23 The Rees Home Church 225
24 The Judson Wade Reese Family 233
25 The True Lincoln Reese Family. 249
26 The Angeline Reese Zieger Family 263
27 The Ann Adelle Reese Huntly Family. . . . 283

PART VII — EPILOGUE

28 Wales Today 287
    Bibliography. 295

Acknowledgments

IF THERE is any achievement within these pages, it is due to the dedicated efforts of so many who saw reflections in the mirror of time that revealed an enlightened and honorable pioneer ancestry. Most all of their work, as well as this final copy, was done before and without the use of the modern technology of the Internet or the use of Web sites. We wish to acknowledge the following:

Our friend and confidant, Ms. Boots Kenney of Adventure Travel, whose "Celtic jolitie of spirit" has given encouragement. She also has a grandmother with the Rhys (Rees) name. Her Adventure Travel motto might be the old Welsh saying, "He who stays home, learns nothing."

Several researchers and historians in the Rees (Reese) family in America who have been helpful and have published their findings. Among them are:

Genevieve Beall Porter—*The Reese Family in Michigan*, 1965,
    published in *Michigan Heritage*

William Race & John Powers—*The Rees/Race Family in America*
    available to members of Rees/Race Family Association

Bertha B. Alderidge—*Gillet Families,* 1955

Mary E. Reese—*Genealogy of the Reese Family,* 1903, of the Sir David Rees (Reese) family coming in 1700 to Delaware and then to Pennsylvania

Esther E. Latham—*Families of Gillet,* 1953

Others have written letters that are of record or in direct correspondence with the author. Among them are:

Grace M. Steeves, letters to the author and to others that are in the archives of Newberry Library, Chicago (Reese file #97)

Rev. Harold Reese, to the author over a period of years

Joyce Reese, to the author over the many years from 1966 in regard to the family tree of the Judson Wade Reese family

Jacqueline Reid of Alabama for picture and True L. Reese family data

Rev. Philip Reese for an extensive collection of Reese family tree data

Elinor Zeiger Morlock, for correspondence relating to Gillett acquaintances and their ancestors

C. Richard (Dick) Moffatt for an interesting personal discussion at his home in 2002 and his many contributions to the history recorded in *West Stockbridge, Massachusetts 1774–1974 (9)*

Then, close to home, a thank you to my wife, Barbara, for her unlimited support and encouragement.

Thank you also to my sister-in-law, Peggy Johnson, who spent many hours typing and retyping the manuscript from my hand-written originals and offered helpful suggestions.

Most of all, credit goes to my talented and faithful nephew, Jim Johnson, who, even with certain disabilities, worked long hours to design the cover and interior pages and prepared the entire book for printing.

Also of considerable value were the library services and historical reference materials of the Broward County Library, Community College Branch in Coconut Creek, Florida.

Thanks to Jeffrey L. Thomas whose fine Welsh castle photographs appear in chapter 14.

And to the many thoughtful people with encouraging comments.

—Robert L. Johnson, Author
Harbert, MI

Preface

IT IS a privilege as well as a humbling experience to research and write of a line of ancestors with a name prominent in the medieval history of the Welsh people, as well as pioneers in the early Westward Movement from New York and New England.

Family gatherings leave cherished memories and childhood memories are a spark that can initiate a discussion or an essay. In this case, the Reese Family Reunions stand out to remind us of the moral strength and positive impressions shown by these people with a common ancestry. They fit the mold of an enlightened people.

A concerted effort was made to trace the family back to its Welsh roots. If this turns out to be less definitive than might be hoped for, it will give another researcher an opportunity to visit the National Library of Wales in the university city of Aberystwyth, to trace the name in the sixteenth century, including the children of our "proverbial ancestor," Rhys ap Thomas. With the hope that it will benefit future researchers of the Rhys/Reese family history, I have looked at the big picture. In such a landscape there are endless points of interest. Libraries contain an abundance of information on Wales and its European neighbors. Our study has used a large number of reference materials. Some points of special interest will repeat themselves.

Our inquiry presents more detail of a personal nature as we progress from ancient times to modern day talents and accomplishments. The enormity of the task led to a limitation of family tree data collection and presentation, a huge task in itself.

One of the pleasures gained from an undertaking of this magnitude are the bits of wisdom other writers have wished to pass on, such as:

> True happiness is knowing who you
> are, knowing from where you came,
> having something to do, having some-
> one to love, and to have faith that
> gives you hope for the future.
> —Ancient Welsh saying

> With the perseverance of the Saints, you can be an Achiever, not just a Receiver.
> —Author unknown

The aging French author, Francois, Duc de La Roehefoucauld (1613–1680) said,

> In aging, one becomes more foolish
> and more wise.

Sir Isaac Newton, one of the greatest scientists of all time, said,

> If I have seen further than others, it is
> because I have stood on the shoulders
> of giants.

On the Wales Cymru plaque (p. xv), the saying is:

> A man who stays at home learns
> nothing.

Our prayer is like that of Ruth Bell Graham from her book, *Love Looks Beyond*,

> God, help us to see beyond the now
> to the before and note with tenderness what lies between—and love the
> more.

And on a final note, Thomas Wolfe stated, "You can't go home again."

It probably means that we can't recapture our youth. There is, however, a place where we can go again and again. Like a precious time capsule, it contains all our dreams and hopes. It is called Memory.

If this narrative causes the reader to imagine and possibly understand the hopes and dreams of our ancestors, it will not have been written in vain.

—Robert L. Johnson
September 2005

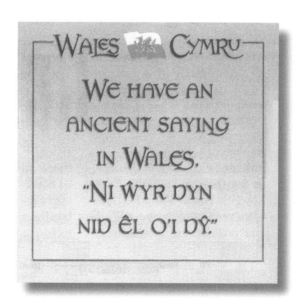

WALES *Cymru—"Land of Fellow Countrymen"*

The identifying icon for the following section, *Part I—Introduction*, is the Royal Coat of Arms of Sir Rhys ap Tewdwr, king of Southwest Wales in 1093, the earliest coat of arms with the Rhys surname.

PART I

Introduction

1

CHRONOLOGY OF EVENTS
IN RELATED HISTORY

SOME of the great events shaping the history of Europe and the lives of our ancestors can help us to understand our heritage as well as trace their movement from the middle ages to the early years of American history. Personal identification also changes from the single, simple name of medieval times to a name and relationship and then to the present day system of a Christian name with a surname. A study of the great events leads to the conclusion that turbulent times arrive at about five hundred year intervals, from the birth of Christ.

55 B.C.	Julius Caesar conducts reconnaissance raid across the channel to British Isles
A.D. 43	A Roman legion of 40,000 men occupies the British Isles
383	Magnus Maximus and many Roman troops leave Britain to press his claim as Emperor
410	There is no longer a Roman presence in Wales
436	Roman troops leave the British Isles
476	Start of the Middle Ages (often called Dark Ages)
844–877	Rhodri the Great—ruler of Wales
910–950	Howel the Good—ruler of all Wales
1039–1063	Gruffudd ap Llywelyn—ruler of all Wales
1046	Gruffudd the king fought 36 Viking ships from Ireland
1052	Rhys, the Welsh king's brother was killed
1063	King Gruffudd killed by his own men on August 5
1066	Battle of Hastings won by William the Conqueror (Norman)
1066–1154	Norman kings rule Britain
1078–1093	Rhys ap Tewdwr—ruler of South Wales (fell to Normans)
1081–1137	Grufudd ap Cynan—ruler of North Wales

1137–1170 Owain Gwynedd—ruler of some provinces of Wales

1155–1197 Rhys ap Gruffudd—ruler of some provinces of Wales

1154–1399 Plantagenet—English Royal House

1194–1240 Llywelyn ap Iorwerth (the Great)

1240–1246 Llywelyn ap David

1255–1283 Llywelyn ap Gruffudd (Prince of Wales—Llywelyn the last)

1272–1307 Edward I rules as King of England

1277–1282 The war against Wales by Edward I

1337–1422 Hundred Years War in Europe

1348 The Black Death Plague rages in France

1359–1415 Owain Glyndwr, Prince of Wales leads revolt

1413 Rhys ap Thomas appointed Sheriff of Carmaethan

1438 Johann Gutenberg invented printing by moveable type

1449 Sir Rhys ap Thomas born, grandson of Sheriff

1460–1485 Wars of the Roses

1484 Reformer Zwingli born in Switzerland

1478 Sir Thomas More born

1485 End of the Middle Ages

CAREW CASTLE
a Rhys castle near Pembroke, Pembrokeshire, south Wales (p. 117)

1485–1609	Reign of House of Tudor: Henry VII, Henry VIII, Edward VI, Lady Jane Grey, Mary I, and Elizabeth I
1509	John Calvin born in France
1517	Start of the Protestant Reformation
1519	Zwingli made Vicar of Zurich Cathedral
1521	Martin Luther excommunicated by Roman Catholic Church
1529	Ottoman Empire at height of power
1525	Rhys ap Thomas dies
1531	Zwingli executed
1531	Rhys ap Gruffudd executed (grandson and heir of Rhys ap Thomas)
1533	King Henry VIII marries Anne Boleyn
1534	Sir Thomas More committed to the Tower of London on April 17
1534	Sir Thomas More executed on July 6
1535	John Calvin flees Paris
1535	Parliament abolishes authority of the Pope
1536	Articles of Faith written for a Church of England
1536	Catherine of Argonne (discarded wife of Henry VIII) dies of cancer
1536	Act of Union, Wales with England (including Marches)

1536	English used in Welsh courts (replaces Welsh language)
1538	Execution of unruly Marcher Lords
1540	Six executions: three Reformers and three Catholics, for denying the supremacy of King Henry VIII. (This was the beginning of the Church of England.)
1545–1563	Council of Trent reexamines Catholic Church doctrine.
1547	Ivan the Terrible crowned Czar of Russia
1549	Explorers from Netherlands, Italy, Spain, and Portugal increase their nations' circles of power
1553	Mary Tudor crowned Queen of England
1555	Bloody Mary begins persecution of Protestants
1555	Bishop Thomas Cranmer executed (burned at the stake)
1558	Elisabeth I crowned
1562	The massacre of Hugenots at Vassy by Guise troops
1564	John Calvin dies; is buried in an unmarked grave
1567–1573	Spanish Duke of Alva responsible for persecution and deaths of more than 100,000 Christians in the Netherlands
1572	Massacre of St. Batholomew's Day (8/24) in Paris and all of France

KIDWELLY CASTLE
a Rhys castle in Dyfed, south Wales (p. 109)

1588	Spain sends Armada to invade England
1598	Edict of Nautes issued by Henry IV of France granting two forms of worship and allowing Hugenots places in society
1604	James I makes peace with Spain
1608	Pilgrims move to the Netherlands
1609–1714	House of Stuart rules England
1609	Mary Stuart, Queen of Scots crowned queen
1617	Pilgrims decide to leave for America
1618–1648	European Thirty Years War; German provinces devastated
1620	Pilgrims leave for America; arrive November 11 after sixty-six days
1685	Hugenots go to Germany, Switzerland, England, and Netherlands
1714–1901	House of Hanover rules England
1901–to date	House of Windsor rules England

CILGERRAN CASTLE
a Rhys castle in Cardigan, Pembrokeshire, Wales (p. 112)
Original photo © Jan Kohl, www.castlesofwales.org

2

THE NAME

RHYS TO REESE

RHYS is a Welsh name in the native language. The name appears frequently in Welsh genealogies. Rhys translated to English is Rees. Rhys pronounced in English is "Rice" or "Rhice." Rees pronounced in German and Dutch sounds like "Race" in English.

The Rees name means "ardor" (17) which in turn embraces warmth, eloquence, emotion, zeal, fervor, and love, all of which may be found in music, poetry, academia, and the ministry. These qualities form the spirit of the Rees legacy.

Rhys is also known to be an ancient Celtic or Roman name. One authority believes the name, as well as the Welsh names of

Owian and Emrys, may be the names of Roman soldiers who stayed in Wales after the main force withdrew in the early 5th century. The Rhone and Rhine rivers have a similar Roman-Celtic origin

Wales has been a land of few surnames. Prior to the Industrial Revolution there were far less than a hundred surnames (family names). Surnames were introduced into Wales following the Acts of Union in 1536, making an identifiable family name a requirement of the English legal system (17).

Inhabitants of the sparsely populated "straggling" settlements of Wales had no need to adopt surnames, though the estate-centered gentry of the 16th century soon accepted them. Of course, the Welsh system of naming was distinctive—by patronymics or abbreviated genealogies rather than the Anglo-Saxon system of surnames (12).

The Welsh had a tradition of identifying a person with a given name followed by the father's name, preceded by an "ap" meaning "son of" or an "ach" meaning "daughter of," the latter being seldom used. With the father's name changing from generation to generation, it becomes difficult to trace family relationships. A name that is used in every other or alternate generation, or predominates in a lineage, most often winds up as the surname coming from that ancestral line. One example: Owen ap Thomas has a son named Thomas (son of Owen) who in turn has a son he names Owen (son of Thomas). One of these names will, at the families' choosing, become the surname. Another example: although Prys may become Price in English, it is also common for ap (son of) Rhys to become Price and ap Richard to become Prichard or even "ap" can be "ab" making "ab Rhys" translated to Bresse (16). In the line of the Rees family coming to Michigan from West Stockbridge, Massachusetts, Johannes kept his father's surname, whereas his brother Nicholas chose to use the Race name (9). A good family name may serve as a badge of honor, and for most people it is their most treasured possession (16).

Most of the Welsh immigrants of the 19th and 20th centuries, coming directly from their homeland, chose to modify their Rees name by adding an "e." Some chose to further change their name to Reece. The sons of Jacob and Sylvia House Rees of Milton Township, Michigan chose to add the "e" to their surnames.

A study of Welsh names is like no other in Western culture. It presents a challenge to first of all, the linguist, then the historian and genealogist. By the 19th century English, Norman, and Biblical Christian names had almost completely replaced some of the more resonant Welsh names (16).

3
A COAT OF ARMS

ERALDRY has been referred to as the "floral border in the garden of European history" and as a "picturesque record of the achievements and courage of past leaders of the people." In the Middle Ages it was the exclusive domain of kings, knights and nobility. Heraldry was well developed by the 13th century with rules and terminology, which has been the basis for its laws and language through the centuries. Specialists in the field are known as heralds.

Originally, a herald was a messenger and maker of proclamations. His function in the medieval battlefield related to communications. When helmets hid the wearer's face, it was necessary to wear a distinctive coat (a mantle) or to display a flag for identification. This eventually became the coat of arms.

Although symbolic and decorative, heraldry was a symbol of family unity and the obligations and duties of those who were a part of this basic unit of society (13).

The coat of arms in the British Isles are often associated with the elevation to knighthood of a son of nobility or one who has shown courage in battle. In more recent times, knighthood is conferred upon those who have had great accomplishments in their chosen profession and are given the title of "Sir."

There are a number of coats of arms with the Rees surname. The earliest is the Royal Coat of Arms of Rhys ap Tewdwr, king of Southwest Wales in 1093. It may also have belonged to Rhys ap Gruffudd, Lord of Southwest Wales reigning from 1132 to 1197. The shield has a partition line called "indented" (sawtooth) outlining a gold border (Fig. 3.1).

FIGURE 3.1 Royal Coat of Arms of Rhys ap Tewdwr

The charge is a lion rampart. No motto, crest, mantle, or helmet is associated with this escutcheon as displayed in the Mullins of London *Heraldic Scroll*.

The arms of Sir Rhys ap Thomas as noted in the *Annals* (51) by Thomas Nicholas, was simply described as—"argent, a chevron sable between three ravens." The shield pictured here from Mullins of London, shows the chevron with ermine pattern as used in heraldry.

After 1536 when English became the official, or court language of Wales, a number of Sir Rhys' offspring took the surname Rice. The raven used in this *achievement of arms* (Fig. 3.2) is a bold, quick-sighted bird. A sentiment of veneration or superstition is often attached to it. Although nearly extinct in some places, it is fed and provided for around the Tower of London. The raven measures about 26 inches in length and has a wingspan of three feet. It is entirely black, its feathers having a purple iridescence. The bards of the time often spoke of Sir Rhys as the *raven* or as *three ravens*.

The Rees coat of arms (Fig. 3.3) was taken from a chart prepared by the American Historical Society in 1928 at the request of Mrs. Lewis Singer Gillette, the daughter of Nancy M. Rees and Mahlon Gillette. It is described as: "arms—azure, two chevrons with blue and gold and mantle with blue and gold flowing artwork, with late form barred helmet and breastplate." The complete chart (Fig. 3.7) is shown on page 15 as found in the Rare Book Room of the Library of Congress, *Gillette and Allied Families* CS G475.

The frontispiece in the book *The Genealogy of the Reese Family* by Mary E. Reese, published in Richmond, VA in 1903, depicts another coat of arms, quartered and showing the Reese name changes (Fig. 3.4). The quarters represent parents, grandparents, etc., which can go

FIGURE 3.2
RICE coat of arms

FIGURE 3.3
REES coat of arms

FIGURE 3.4
REESE coat of arms

FIGURE 3.5
REES family crest

FIGURE 3.6
BARON REES
coat of arms

on indefinitely. The Mary Reese work is based on her family, the Rev. David Reese, who came to Philadelphia after 1700.

In the archives of the DAR Library in Washington D.C., the author found a Rees family crest, as shown here (Fig. 3.5), dated 1599. It is obviously of Welsh origin. It would appear appropriate for, or possibly come from, the Coat of Arms of Sir Rhys ap Thomas which often was found with a very limited description. In *Burke's Peerage and Baronetage* there is another coat of arms with a Rees name, the Baron Rees, Co. Gwent (Peter Wynford Innes Rees) (Fig. 3.6). Baron Rees is a descendent of the Rev. Thomas Morgan Rees, born November 6, 1850. The baron, born December 9, 1926, is also known as the Rt. Honorable Lord Rees. The coat of arms has been amplified through the generations to date.

It would appear that much more could be found in regard to this very interesting subject.

Chapter 3—A Coat of Arms 15

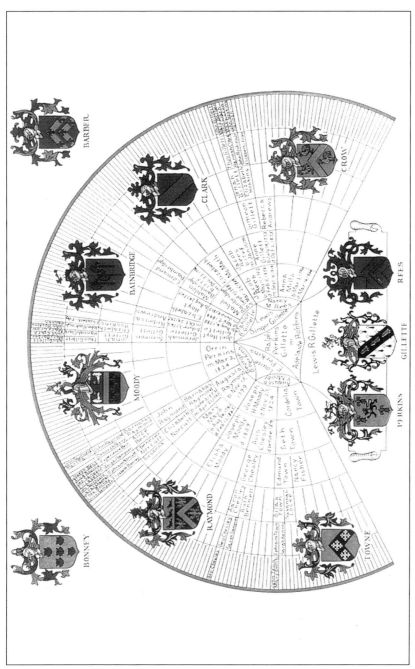

FIGURE 3.7
Gillette and Allied Families CS G475

WALES
Cymru—"Land of Fellow Countrymen"

The identifying icon for the following section, *Part II—A Historical Perspective,* is the Celtic Cross with its distinctive circular halo surrounding the crosspieces which has been said to symbolize eternity.

PART II
A Historical Perspective

4
THE CELTS

THE CELTS were an ancient people of southern European climes who moved north, settling in Gaul, and later as the climate moderated, in Brittany and the British Isles. The earliest known Celts (called "Celtae" by Caesar) were of barbaric origin, sacking Rome in about 390 B.C. and Delphi in 278 B.C. According to history, the Roman army had subdued Celtic settlements in Gaul by 52 B.C. It is believed there was no great influx of peoples into the British Isles during the Iron Age, which came to northwest Europe about 1000 B.C. or before. The original Celtic tongue, an Indo-European language, came to the Isles prior to that time and developed in different ways in Ireland, Wales, Brittany, and England.

Elements of the Celtic language and culture have been identified in Europe and as far east as Galatia and Anatolia in present day Turkey. The names of the rivers Rhone, Rhine, and Danube and the cities, London, Paris, and Vienna, are Celtic names. It may be noted here that the diphthong "Rh" in Rhine and Rhone and common in the Welsh language, is also in the surname "Rhys."

The Welsh consider theirs the land of the bards and the last bright jewel of King Arthur's crown, fiercely guarding the ancient Brythonic language spoken at King Arthur's court.

Although the Celtic-Welsh of today are often thought of as having normal height and dark hair, the barbarian Celtic chieftains were tall and fair-skinned with blond hair and blue eyes. They wore flowing ear-to-ear mustaches and swept back hair. Their druids, or priests, were recruited from the children of their chieftains (8).

The Celts held the spoken word in high regard and their myths, legends, and traditions were transmitted orally. Next to the king, or warlord, the most important figures in Celtic society were the druid and the bard, or poet. The druids (denwydd in Welsh) were seers with an intimate knowledge of the natural world. They could be either men or women and were shamans, mediators, knowers, and keepers of wisdom. All their lore was memorized and passed down verbally. They acted as both priests and judges.

There were many legends of heroes and heroines. The Celtic heroes were role models for the Celtic warrior. Cuchulainn, the champion warrior of Ulster, who filled his chariot with the heads of enemies was a larger than life rowdy. The authority of the Welsh chieftain, Pwy II, extended into the mystic "other world." The code of honor that Pwy I followed linked him with the heroic figure of King Arthur and the numerous legends of the Round

Table, which later became popular medieval romances.

Celtic heroes often learned the arts of war from warrior women, and it was the mother who would name and arm the warrior. Cuchulainn, for example, was sent to Skye to learn the arts of war from Scathach, a warrior goddess. The heroines of Celtic myths enjoyed power and commanded armies in their own right, as did the historical Queen Boudicea, who led a revolt against Roman rule in first century Britain. Warrior Queen Maeve of Connacht was believed to hold the kingdom's sovereignty in her person, and no king could reign there unless he was married to her (40).

There is both joy and sorrow in Celtic myths which reflect the reality of life, and the Celt is nothing if not a realist. Then in a different vein, wisdom, inspiration, and the gift of prophecy could be bestowed by inhabitants of the "other world," often in miraculous cauldrons containing magical potions. Sometimes the cauldron was a vessel which fed everyone, and at other times it was a huge pot that brought dead warriors back to life. Later, in Christian times, it became the Holy Grail, identified with the chalice of Jesus' Last Supper. The great poet and prophet, Taliesin, came to his bardic illumination after sipping inspiration—the Celts called it "Awen"—from the forbidden cauldron of the goddess Coridwen. Another seer was Myrddin, who appears in the Arthurian stories as Merlin, and who was a legendary figure of the Welsh town of Carmarthen (Caerfyrddin) which means "Merlin's City." The Welsh city of Caerleon, which was fortified by the Romans, has been referred to as the location of Camelot with King Arthur and his legendary Round Table.

In Celtic culture, the spiritual and material worlds were interconnected and humanity was a part of nature, each being enriched by the other. The relationship also meant that the land did not belong to the people but that the people belonged to the land.

The pagan religion or beliefs were filled with fear and evidence of human sacrifice. The human head was a symbol for the Celts of divine power and, as the seat of the soul, a link with the ancestral spirit. During times of war, the severed heads of enemies were collected and fixed to the doorposts of forts and houses. It was thought that the heads protected the buildings, a belief that persisted well into the medieval period. The head of the legendary British King, Bran the Blessed, was cut off by his own troops after his defeat in Ireland, and continued to eat and speak during the voyage home. By tradition it was buried in London and still lies under the Tower of London, protecting Britain from invasion. Needless to say, there was little of what we know as civilization in the era prior to the advent of Christ.

The sober Christianity of Patrick and the wild paganism of the Celts, according to one Irish writer, fit the dual influences of his boyhood. Another very attractive personality of the early Celtic church is Dewi Sant (St. David). The Welsh celebrate St. David's Day every March 1. Like Patrick, he was not made a saint by the Roman Catholic Church. St. David and St. Patrick will be discussed in another chapter, along with another notable personality, known as "Holy Rhys," with an influence on the Welsh people at a later time.

In the Middle Ages the Celts were driven to the western fringes of the British Isles and Brittany and are the forebears of many of the present day Welsh people.

Chapter 4—The Celts   21

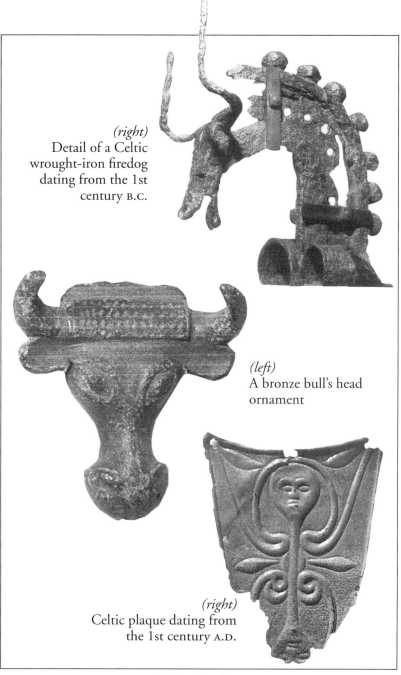

(right)
Detail of a Celtic wrought-iron firedog dating from the 1st century B.C.

(left)
A bronze bull's head ornament

(right)
Celtic plaque dating from the 1st century A.D.

FIGURE 4.1
Early Celtic Art

5
THE BRITONS

AMONG the early Celtic tribes in the British Island group was the Brythons for whom Britain is named. The island people, now numbering over 60 million, are from many backgrounds: Germanic, Angles, Saxons, Jutes, Danes, and Norsemen who, over time, invaded the islands in the 5th century. These vigorous, sometimes fierce, farmers, hunters and fisherman established small kingdoms. The Celtic remnant were driven west out of the island's fertile midlands to Wales, Cornwall and across the channel to Brittany. The Welsh then became the prime defender of the Brythonic language, which developed in different ways among the peoples of Ireland, Wales, Scotland and England. The resultant Welsh language soon became unique, differing from all other spoken and written communications.

With the advent of Christianity developing by the 5th century, the seed was planted for Britain to become the builder of the world's most far-flung empire, pioneering in free speech, social welfare, democracy as well as the birthplace of world leaders, great scientists, explorers and writers.

Roman invaders led by Julius Caesar first arrived in 55 B.C. and by A.D. 43 had conquered most of the area of England. They built roads, forts, cities and Hadrians Wall in the north to keep out the rebellious Picts, a non-Celtic tribe driven north by the invading Romans. The fearsome Picts became united with the Caedonians of the north and the Scotti who migrated from Ulad (Northern Ireland) prior to the 9th century.

The Romans did not claim Ireland. They had military control over Britain as far as Hadrians Wall and for a time up to the Antonine Wall planned for a line from present day Edinburg to Glasgow. The Romans began leaving in A.D. 407 to defend interests in Gaul leaving Britain as easy prey. In A.D. 410 Emperor Honorius told Britain to provide for their own defense.

Offa's Dyke, started in 716, is named for King Offa of Mercia, who reigned 757–796 and completed in 784 as a well defined boundary with Wales following his attacks in 780 and 784.

In 865 the Danish Vikings "Great Army" invaded Britain but were confined by Alfred the Great, King of West Saxons. He became king of all England in 871. As king, he encouraged education and established an army and navy. The Norman's, formerly called "Norsemen" who first came to England to plunder and enslave it, gradually mixed with the Anglo-Danish population. Edward the Confessor, whose mother was from Normandy, assumed the throne in 1042 and built the forerunner of Westminster Abbey. As the last royal Saxon to rule England, Edward left only a young boy to succeed him. The Saxon governing body, the "witan," passed over the youth and chose his brother-in-law, Harold, (b. 1003, r. 1066) Earl of Wessex to succeed him.

This led to a rivalry—King Harold III of Norway and William, Duke of Normandy, Edward's cousin—competing for England's throne in 1066. The Norwegians attacked from the north and were vanquished by Harold's mounted infantry. Harold hastened south and was defeated at Hastings by William. Harold was killed by an arrow to his brain. The well-trained Norman army of 12,000 conquered England, a land of over 1.5 million people, in a historical battle. William was crowned king at Westminster on Christmas Day, 1066, a date long remembered in Britain.

After defeating some rebellious Saxons by 1070, William was not only a conqueror, but also a brutal and experienced soldier as well as an expert in administration. He made the dukedoms strictly hereditary, which became a characteristic of the English, monarchy. *The Doomsday Book* made from a 1086 survey indicates the level of control William had gained over the island. His bureaucracy was operated by his servants, often churchmen, and the Norman rulers were from the royal houses of Europe, often referred to as restless and aggressive.

William the Conqueror's youngest son Henry I, reigned from 1100 to 1135 following the accidental death of his brother, William Rufus, who reigned 1087–1100. He also claimed Normandy, which belonged to his elder brother Robert.

Like the Romans, the Norman's were builders. The Tower of London was begun in William's time. Soon after, Westminster Hall and some 50 castles and many churches and cathedrals were built. While Offa's Dyke marked the end of Anglo-Saxon annexation of Welsh territory, the situation was shattered in the 11th century by the arrival of the Norman's who conquered the border zone in Wales, known as the *Marches* (a French term meaning "frontier"). Over time a hybrid society developed in the area as the Welsh, Anglo-Saxon, and Norman peoples and cultures mixed together (25). These as well as the Scottish semi-autonomous border areas were established as buffer zone earldoms. Strong leaders arose in Wales, Scotland, and Ireland. Scotland emerged eventually as a separate kingdom.

Under Henry II, a great grandson of William and the first of the Plantagenet Dynasty, which ruled Britain from 1154 to 1399, the first universities at Oxford and Cambridge were established. In 1265 the Curia Regis became the first parliament and met in the new Westminster Hall.

Two sons—Richard the Lion-hearted, a popular hero, killed in 1199, and John—followed Henry. Richard led the first crusade to the Holy Land in 1189. In 1215 the unpopular King John was forced by English barons and the church to accept the Magna Carta, an important document listing the fundamental rights of all Englishmen. It was basically written to limit the power of despotic kings who in the Middle Ages believed they ruled by divine right.

Edward I, ruling 1272–1307, spent eight years before crushing Welsh uprisings in 1295. In November 1276 he resolved to force the Welsh Prince Llywylyn into submission. He began the war by appointing a number of Marcher lords as his royal officials in Wales. With the fall of Dynefwr Castle in April 1277, the local ruler, Rhys ap Maredudd switched his allegiance to the English. Unfortunately for Prince Llywelyn, he was not the last to defect. Llywelyn's brother Daffydd was an ally of the king and received lands for his loyalty. The king's brother, Edmund "Crouchback" of Lancaster led troops into the region of Ceredigion on the West Coast. Over half of the king's force were

Welsh. The Welsh princes who had deserted Llywelyn out of resentment for his overbearing style, soon found life under Edward's rule to be even more intolerable. In the detailed account (33) by Paul V. Walsh, the revolt led Edward in March 1282 not only to "put an end to the malice of the Welsh as originally planned, but to conquer native Wales."

Llywelyn, often referred to as "Llywelyn the Last," was killed along with 3,000 of his men in December 1282. His head was sent to Edward who had it dispatched to London where it was displayed above one of the gates leading to the Tower. On September 30, 1294 Welsh soldiers in the king's army mutinied, killing their English officers. A cousin of Prince Llywelyn, Madog ap Llywelyn, rallied the loyal and discontented Welsh, however, by late July the English had put down the last of the rebels and Madog was imprisoned in the Tower of London.

For 400 years the English kings tried to retain lands on the continent causing wars with the French, including the 100 Years War begun in 1337 by Edward III. He coveted all of France. Despite some victories, Edward became convinced he could not win the French crown. In the Peace of Bretigny in 1360 he got Calais, areas of southern France and by the war's end in 1453, the English held only Calais. It was a peasant girl, Joan of Arc, who led the French to victory at Orleans.

During this time, 1348–1349, the Black (bubonic) Plague reduced England's population from about 4 million to a little over 2 million. The great labor shortage resulted in higher wages and an increasing number of "freemen." By 1385 grammar schools were teaching the English of common people, which won over the French spoken by nobility and the Latin by the clergy. The Norman's had considerable influence over the development of the English language.

The Wars of the Roses broke out in 1455 with the Battle of St. Albans after the House of York decided to oust the weak Henry VI of the House of Lancaster. He ruled since a child a year old. Henry's reign was considered a political disaster for England even though he founded Eton and King's College at Cambridge. As an honest and gentle king living a simple life with benefactions to the Roman Catholic Church, he was suggested as a candidate for canonization by the Church.

The Wars of the Roses involved the nobility related to royal cousins of the descendants of two of Edward III's younger sons; John of Gaunt, the Duke of Lancaster and Richard, Duke of York. The heraldic symbol of the Lancastrians was a red rose while the Yorkists' symbol was a white rose. The prize was to be the throne. The common people were not involved to any extent, the country was not devastated, and business continued as the nobility was decimated. Losers were beheaded and survivors confiscated their estates.

Henry VI was deposed and murdered in the Tower of London and was succeeded by Edward IV, the Duke of York. Edward died in 1483 and was succeeded by Richard III, his brother, another unpopular king. Richard was killed in 1485 in the Battle of Bosworth Field. The victor was Henry Tudor, age 28, Earl of Richmond, born in Pembroke Castle. He was of the Welsh Tudors and an heir of the House of Lancaster. One writer, (4) claims Rhys ap Thomas killed Richard III at Bosworth Field.

Henry VII ended the Wars of the Roses by marrying Edward IV's daughter, Elizabeth, uniting the Houses of Lancaster and York.

Along with the century of the Tudors came great changes in the world which seemed to be every 500 years of history since the birth of Christ and the northern conquests of the Celts and

Romans. The next age saw the fall of the Roman Empire around 500; then the time of the Vikings, Norsemen, and Normans at the turn of the millennium. Now, in the 15th century comes the Age of the Reformation, the printing press, Bible translations and other great literature, and the age of world-wide exploration. This was also the beginning of the century of the Tudors with two of England's most influential rulers.

The first was the notorious King Henry VIII (Fig. 5.1), the extravagant, ruthless husband of six wives and father of three monarchs. He tangled with the Pope over who should be the head of the Church of England. Following his excommunication by Rome, he seized the property of the Catholic Church, which owned a quarter of England. He sold it to finance his exploits. Much writing of his reign was focused on his six wives as noted by Derek Wilson's (18) *In the Lions Court* introduction. The tragic comings and goings of three Catherines, two Annes and a Jane, is summed up in the mantra:

> Divorced, beheaded, died
> Divorced, beheaded, survived.

Was he the king of beasts in Wilson's story of "power, ambition and sudden death in the reign of Henry VIII?" Sir Thomas More (Fig. 5.1) has written in his *Utopia* that his entering royal service "was a spiritual bed of nails," in the court of Henry VIII. More was executed in 1535. Thomas Cromwell, Archbishop and a minister on the staff of the king, was executed the same day the king married Catherine Howard, July 28, 1540. Many other people, including Bishop John Fisher (1460–1535) (Fig. 5.1) were executed when they were no longer useful to the king, or opposed his slightest whims. Also executed was the grandson of Rhys ap Thomas.

An amazing thing about Henry was that he never lost his

instinct for the nation itself. Although feared, he was popular and never compromised his policy to see England thrive as no other state in Europe. This history of Tudor England is unparalleled in many respects. Wales was incorporated into England in 1536, but remained socially and culturally distinct, even to this day. Wales has its own parliament for Welsh affairs and its own languages, Welsh and English.

Chapter 5—The Britons   31

FIG. 5.1

6
THE WELSH

WALES, as a nation, occupies the western peninsula of Britain, an area of about 8,000 square miles. It is bounded on the north and west by the Irish Sea and on the south by the Bristol Channel. The boundary with England is marked by Offa's Dyke. The original kingdoms in Wales were Gwynedd in the north, Powys in the central to northeast and Deheubarth across the south. The Welsh people are referred to as Cymry, or compatriots, and their country as Cymru, the land of fellow countrymen (Fig. 6.1).

Some of the more notable rulers of Wales in its early history were:

Rhodri Mawr (the Great)	844–876	All Wales
Hywel Dda (the Good)	910–950	All Wales
Llywelyn ap Seisyll	?–1022	All Wales

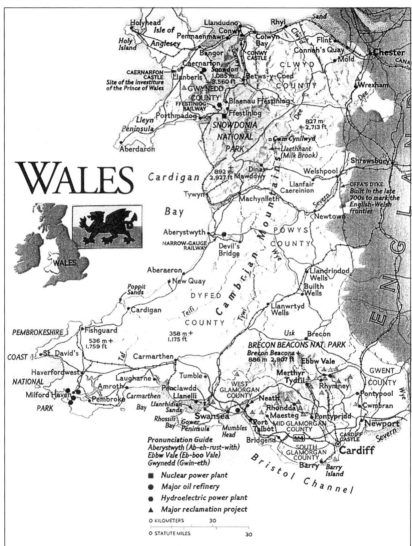

THE WELSH derive their name from the Anglo-Saxon Wallas, for "foreigh." More apt is the native name, Cymru, for "the land of fellow countrymen"—since their Celtic forebears had already endured three centuries of Roman rule before the Anglo-Saxons overran England in the fifth century A.D. The Welsh resisted them from mountain strongholds, but fared less well under the armor-clad Normans, who in the 12th century began to erect the many stone castles that became the centers of Welsh towns. Paradoxically, it was the ascension of a Welshman, Henry Tudor, to the English throne that led in 1536 to the Act of Union, bonding Wales to England.

FIGURE 6.1
Map of Wales, courtesy of National Geographic (42)

Gruffydd ap Llewelyn	1039–1063	All Wales
Rhys ap Tewdwr (King of Deheubarth)	1078–1093	South Wales
Gruffydd ap Cynan	1081–1137	North Wales
Owain Gwynedd	1137–1170	Some Provinces
Rhys ap Gruffydd (Lord Rhys)	1155–1197	Some Provinces
Llewelyn ap Iorwerth (the Great)	1194–1240	All Wales
Dafydd ap Llewelyn	1240–1246	
Llewelyn ap Gruffydd (the Last)	1255–1282	

Until 1200 Welsh rulers were referred to as kings. At any one time there could be several kings. When the nation had only Gwynedd and Deheubarth kingdoms, they were ruled by princes.

The 9th and 10th centuries witnessed a period of savage coastal attacks in the south by Danish and Norse pirates (Vikings). These attacks led the early kings to cooperate with and unite the small kingdoms under their authority (4).

Wales was a power under Gruffudd ap Llewelyn in the mid-eleventh century at the same time Edward the Confessor was the English King (1042–1066). Gruffudd overextended his forces into the March borderlands and was met by Harold, son of Godwine, Earl of Wessex, who pursued and killed him on August 5, 1063 in the Snowdonia area (3).

Harold married Gruffudd ap Llewelyn's widow, Ealdgyth, the only woman to be both queen of Wales and England. Her grandmother was Lady Godiva. Harold replaced the ineffective

Edward the Confessor on the throne, an election that disregarded the claims of Edward's heirs and vague claim of William, Duke of Normandy. The rivalry was settled on Senlac Hill October 14, 1066, near Hastings after an eight-hour battle (3). William the Conqueror seized the kingdom of England and became William I.

William I tried to deal with the Welsh by setting up border earldoms to protect his newly won kingdom from their incursions. The power of the border earls (Marches) grew steadily. Only after the death of Rhys ap Tewdwr (1093) did the Anglo-Norman Barons take full possession of the Vale of Glamorgan in southern Wales (58).

Like the Romans, the Normans were builders. They built many motte and bailey (earthwork and wood type) fortifications and castles, most of which are in partial ruin today. They served their purpose in discouraging raids from the Irish, Vikings or Picts, as well as during the conflict with Edward I in the 13th century.

The Welsh, in the age of Lord Rhys (1133–1197), were drawing closer to Latin Europe, which was confident enough to launch Crusades to the Holy Land. A number of Welshmen, including Lord Rhys, expressed a desire to take part. By this time a foreign war was not a new experience for the Welsh. Owain ap Cadwgan was with Henry I's army in Normandy and the first of many Welshmen to serve the kings of England in France. Lord Rhys was fluent in French as well as Welsh but not English. Rhys was known to mingle with members of the House of Clare as if he were a full member of the *Francigenae,* the French-speaking aristocracy which formed the ruling class from Jerusalem to Dublin and all of Europe (3).

Heartland Europe in the 12th century was deeply suspicious of the peoples of the periphery such as the Celts, Slavs, and

Scandinavians. Henry II wrote the Byzantine emperor "The Welsh are a wild people who cannot be tamed." Similar comments have been found in the voluminous writings of Giraldus Cambrensis, often considered an outstanding Welsh patriot. Giraldus was proud of his Welsh decent—being the grandson of Nest, the daughter of Rhys ap Tewdwr (3).

Rhys ap Gruffudd (Lord Rhys), one of the great Welsh leaders of the 12th century, was based at Dinefwr, the Rhys family stronghold. King Henry II seized great tracts of his land in 1157. Rhys fought back and by 1166 had regained most of it and set up a new court at Cardigan. It was here that he convened the first ever *Eisteddfod*.

Llewelyn ap Iorwerth, known as Llewelyn the Great, attempted to set up a Welsh state along feudal, hereditary lines. The English Crown was reluctant to accept the situation. By 1255 Llewelyn's grandson, Llewelyn ap Gruffudd, took control of Gwynedd and in 1258 assumed his grandfather's title of Prince of Wales. Although recognized by Henry III, Llewelyn's problems with rival princes and finances continued to plague him (4).

Llewelyn ap Gruffydd (also spelled Llywelyn) displeased the king in 1265 when he supported the rebellious baron Simon de Montfort against King Henry III and obtained Montfort's recognition as Prince of Wales. That alliance was undone when Henry's son Edward slew Montfort at the Battle of Evesham in 1267 (33).

Upon Edward's succession to the throne in 1274, Llewelyn became concerned as to whether the king would recognize his title as Prince of Wales. Edward demanded that Llewelyn pay homage to him prior to any such recognition. Llewelyn, suspicious of Edward, procrastinated. He was justified when Edward provided sanctuary for Llewelyn's brother, Duffydd ap Gruffydd, and Prince Gruffydd ap Gwenwynwyn, both of whom Llewelyn had expelled for plotting his assassination (33).

On November 12, 1276, King Edward I resolved to force Llewelyn into submission. Author Paul V. Walsh in his *King Edward's Conquest of Wales* for *Military History* (33), in 1999, begins his treatise from the eye of a Welsh scout perched in an oak tree.

> A path more than a bowshot wide was being cleared through the woods. Making its way through this clearing was an endless column of warriors displaying a sea of brilliant colors that stood in stark contrast to the dull autumn sky. Prominent among the lead group was a nobleman, over six feet tall, towering above his comrades. He appeared to be in his late thirties. His face was comely, though flawed by a drooping left eyelid, above which hung a few dirty blond curls peeking out beneath a crown. This was Edward I, King of England.

Mr. Walsh has a Masters Degree in Military History from Temple University and writes with great interest and understanding of the times and military details. He makes history a most attractive subject.

The English imported 100 larger breeds of war horses from France in 1277 as an addition to those maintained by knights supporting the king. England, with a population of at least four million, could raise many more troops than Wales with an estimated 300,000 population (33).

Llewelyn, with his limitations in mind, chose to rely on traditional strategy of using the rugged Welsh terrain to elude the more powerful English rather than confront them in open battle. Edward hoped that the simultaneous summer assault of the three separate forces would overwhelm Llewelyn's outer defenses of Gwyneed. Informed of Edward's plan, Llewelyn sent the Bishop of Bangor to the king's forces with an offer to negotiate.

Edward refused, believing Llewelyn needed to be taught a lesson and he had the force in place to complete the task. There were 800 horses, 15,600 foot soldiers (including 9,000 Welsh who supported the king) and 1,800 axe men who cleared paths through the woods. The "axmen" deprived Llewelyn's troops cover from which to harass Edward's army (33). Another rich source of information on this and other conflicts with the English is given by Philip Warner in his book, *Famous Welsh Battles (5)*.

After Llewelyn surrendered on November 1, 1277 the king made settlements with his knights as well as Llewelyn's brother Daffydd. The seeds of rebellion soon were becoming evident as the Welsh who had deserted Llewelyn, including his brother, resented the king's style as even more intolerable. On March 21, 1282, Daffydd led a rebellion that retook the fortress at Hawarden by surprise and then seized castle strongholds Ruthin, Dinas Dran, and Dolforwyn. The rebellion did not succeed. Llewelyn was killed in December 1282. His head was sent to Edward at Rhuddlan, who sent it on to London where it was displayed above one of the gates leading to the Tower (33).

The death of Llywelyn the Last, was not going to settle the Welsh conflict. The first person to show his disenchantment was Rhys ap Meredith, Prince of South Wales. Although he had supported Edward, the administrators paid scant heed to Rhys' special position. His land and judicial power were encroached upon.

> Suddenly his anger flared up. He captured Dynevor, Drysllwyn,

Llandovery and Carreg Cennen castles and sent the new administrators packing (5).

Edward decided to fight on "reducing" the northern Welsh castles one by one. Now a fugitive, Daffydd was finally captured on June 21, 1293 by Welshmen in Edward's service. In a public ceremony at Shrewsbury, Daffydd was hanged, drawn, and quartered. His head was sent to join his brother's at the Tower of London (33).

Edward II was born in Caernarvon Castle and reigned 1307–1327. Although he was an incompetent king he had a desire to see justice done. The Black Death arrived in Wales in 1349–50 and killed about a quarter of the inhabitants. This affliction disrupted the pattern of land tenure in the whole of Europe, upsetting the agricultural economy (3).

An open rebellion started in 1400 by Owain ap Glyndwr, a descendant of the royal house of Powys. It initially stemmed from a quarrel over land with his Marcher neighbor, Lord Grey of Ruthin. He took Grey to an English court. The case was dismissed apparently with the words, "what care we for barefoot Welsh dogs?" Henry IV then passed laws forbidding the Welsh from bearing arms, holding public office and land trading in English areas (4).

Supported by many of the Welsh gentry, Glyndwr controlled most of Wales by 1404 and proclaimed himself Prince of Wales. After capturing two prominent fortresses, he began forming alliances with foreign powers including Scotland and France. Things were reversed when the king's son returned as a hero from the Battle of Agincourt in France and defeated the Welsh at Grosmont and Usk. In 1406 Glyndwr retreated north and disappeared. He came as close as any one to uniting his country

(4). The king's son became Henry V in 1413.

Welsh history is well recorded in John Davies *A History of Wales,* first published in English in 1990 (3). John Davies is a native of the Rhondda (Valley) Mid Glamorgan County. He was educated at Trinity College, Cambridge, and at University College, Cardiff. He now lives in Cardiff. The book's 700 pages are "like having all Wales in one's hand" in the words of another Welsh historian, Jan Morris.

Of course Welsh history goes on, still influenced to some extent by those with the Rhys-Rees surname. No other small country has such an eventful history as Wales. In the 15th century Wars of the Roses had an effect on the history of the region. In the 16th century the reign of the Tudors had its effect on the Rhys family history, as shown in continued accounts of a more personal nature.

7
THE LEGENDARY KING ARTHUR

THE UNITY of the Roman Empire was challenged by the time Honorius became the independent Emperor of the west in A.D. 395. Rome itself was falling into the hands of the Gothic forces of Alaric. John Davies, in his highly acclaimed *History of Wales* (3) states, "Romono—British, deprived of the protection of Roman troops, seized power from Honorius' officials in

408. In A.D. 410, Honorius recognized their actions and advised them to make arrangements for defending themselves."

The next centuries have been labeled "The Dark Ages" in history. Little or nothing was written and legends and mysteries prevailed in Britain (3).

The "Great King of the Britons" was discovered to be Camelot's King Arthur (Fig. 7.1), not a legend, but a real king who reigned in the fifth century, according to the leading authority on royal genealogy. Debrett's Peerage was to publish the findings of Geoffrey Ashe after the excavations of a site in Somerset (65).

Christian annalists of the early Middle Ages kept records which briefly listed births and deaths of local saints, plagues, famine, Viking raids, etc. In the British Museum are the "Annals Cambriae" *(The Welsh Annals)* which contain Arthur's first appearance in a written document in Latin. The document reads:

> A.D. 518—The Battle of Badon, in which Arthur carried the cross of our Lord Jesus Christ for three days and three nights on his shoulders, and the Britons were the victors.
>
> A.D. 539—The conflict Camlann, in which Arthur and Medrant perished; and there was a pestilence in Briton and Ireland. (Another source pinpoints the battle and Arthur's death at around A.D. 542.)

There are those who question such entries, however, the last entry in the Welsh Annals is the recorded death of the Welsh King Rhodri ap Hywel Dda in 957, lending some legitimacy to the writings (30).

No other figure has inspired more legends, folk tales and

curiosities, nor given his name to more features of the landscape in Wales, than King Arthur. Geoffrey of Monmouth, a twelfth century historian-novelist, claimed that a grassy mound at Caerleon near Newport, Gwent, in southeast Wales, was the site of Arthur's first court, describing it as populated by hundreds of scholars, astrologers and philosophers as well as many fine knights and ladies (4).

At Caerleon is one of the most revealing Roman sites in Europe and the most important in Wales. It was the location of the Second Augustan Legion from A.D. 75. The amphitheater site is associated in local legends with King Arthur's Round Table (28).

FIGURE 7.1
The Nine "Worthies"
(from left) from Old Testament times: Joshua (conqueror of Canaan), David (King of Israel), and Judas Maccabaeus; from pagan times: Hector (son of Priam of Troy), Julius Caesar, and Alexander the Great; from Christian times: Arthur (flying his heraldic standard three golden crowns), Charlemagne, and Godfrey of Bouillion *(detail from a medieval French manuscript illustration)*

Arthurian legends have had a profound impact on western culture and on British culture in particular. When Henry VII's first son was born, the king made sure that he was born and christened at Winchester, a site identified with Camelot, and that he was named Arthur. Arthur II, it was anticipated, would restore Britain's Golden Age and bring a longed-for peace after the strife of the Wars of the Roses. Arthur died young and Britain got the second son, Henry VIII.

So the legendary King Arthur, like Queen Boudica, has become a symbol of tragic greatness (12).

8
THE WARS OF THE ROSES

AGAIN, we can say that many of the great events in the history of Western Civilization took place around the year 1500, in both the 15th and 16th centuries. The Age of Science was about to become evident, the Age of Exploration was when Christopher Columbus became known as the Last Crusader, claiming a New World for Christianity, and the Spanish Queen. History records this time as the end of the Middle Ages. It was also a troubling time in Britain.

The Wars of the Roses took place in England during the 15th century and is remembered as a bloody vicious struggle for power with the throne as the prize. The wars were a dynastic struggle between the Houses of York and Lancaster and involved only the aristocratic families of these houses and their followers. Both parties accepted the unity of the kingdom and the existing system of government by King, Council, and Parliament. Although power changed hands often, English society in general was relatively stable and prosperous. The frequent battles were brief, decisive at the time and did little to lay waste the land or destroy the sources of wealth (14).

In the Wars of the Roses, Britain was also seen as emerging from the shadow of medieval France that lay over the islands since the Norman Conquest. Although it has been estimated that some 70 noble families became extinct, another 50 new families of nobility were formed, many by their own descendants. There were 12 identified battle locations, taking their names from the locations. The symbols of the red rose for the Lancasterians and the white rose for the Yorkists were chosen some years *after* the wars. The conflicts were largely contained in the thirty-year period of 1455–85.

The knights wore metal armor, as did their horses. The prime weapons were the longbow and lance, although the crossbow, war hammer, or mace, were often found in a knight's possession.

Some Welsh "Marcher barons" were involved in a few battles even though Wales was not united to England until 1536. The last decisive battle of the Wars of the Roses did involve Welsh knights, nobles, and an heir to the throne, the Earl of Richmond, Henry Tudor. The Tudor dynasty had its origin in the Welsh "island" or peninsula of Anglesey. The Earl of Richmond was, in fact, born in Pembroke Castle in southwest Wales.

In the battle of Bosworth Field in central England on August 22, 1485, King Richard III was to defend his throne against Henry Tudor, the Earl of Richmond, who came from exile in France. He landed at Milford Haven on the southern Wales peninsula and with the loyalty of the assembly of knights under the authority of Rhys ap Thomas, he marched across Wales to Bosworth Field.

Many authors of British history deal with this decisive battle, including William Shakespeare. When King Richard III became "unhorsed," according to Shakespeare and others, he exclaimed, "A horse, a horse, my kingdom for a horse!" To many who study this event, it seems clear that Rhys ap Thomas, with his longbow, fired the arrow that killed Richard III. That day Henry Tudor became king and brought in the Tudor Dynasty and one of the greatest periods in British history (27).

Cymru—"Land of Fellow Countrymen"

The identifying icon for the following section, *Part III—The Welsh Culture,* is the Harp, traditional musical instrument of Wales dating from the 9th and 10th centuries.

PART III
The Welsh Culture

9
THE PEOPLE

FOR A person born in Wales of Welsh parents is to belong to the first race of Britons. The British later, however, considered the Welsh foreigners as shown by the meaning of their name. They were in time driven to the western parts of the British Isles and Brittany over the centuries taking their language with them. In many respects they were a peculiar people with a language unlike any other and little understood or ever learned by their neighbors. The basic language was fully developed by the 6th century incorporating the Latin influences of the Roman occupation. As a Celtic language used in the early Briton culture it was also known as a Brythonic tongue.

The Celtic independent personality of the Welsh never united in a political sense to form an empire or even a state, other than possibly Ireland as an island state. It is known, however, that many Welshmen have made good public servants going far in civil and diplomatic services, usually outside Wales (6). Within the country the bureaucrats can be very helpful, however, Welsh politics can often be explained by the desire to be difficult. On a personal basis the Welsh are essentially conservative, however, nationally, when the English vote Conservative, the Welsh will vote Liberal (6).

John Winterson Richards, author of a series of booklets with an irreverent look at the beliefs and foibles of the people of a number of nations (6), makes this observation

> The dominant feature of a Welshman's childhood is his mam (mother). The traditional Welsh mam is a combination of the gentleness of a saint and the degree of flexability usually associated with the average mountain, and a Welsh mountain at that, formed of proper igneous rock—none of your sandstone rubbish.

He also mentions how the different regions can be almost as different as nations and most notably is the contrast between the north and south.

> In general North Walians and South Walians get along like 'a house afire,' the house in question having been bought by a South Walian and set on fire by a North Walian.

The butt of a Welsh joke has to be effete, callow, pompous, ignorant, and nine times out of ten it will be an Englishman, e.g.:

> First Welshman: Excuse me, you look like an Englishman.
> Second Welshman: No, I'm not English—I only look like this because I've been sick."

We may remember from our childhood hearing and quoting a "verse tale" sometimes attributed to Sir Walter Scott (1771–1832):

> Fee Fie Foh Fum,
> I smell the blood of an Englishman;
> Be he alive or be he dead,
> I grind his bones to make my bread.

During a lifetime these were the sentiments of many Scots as well as the Welsh.

The truth is that the Welshman is only happy when he is part of an "Us" having a go at "Them." It can even be Wales against the world or at least against the English (6).

The Welsh are prepared to talk to almost anyone in a friendly manner as if they were an old and dear friend, even routinely on public transportation. The English, they note in places like the London Underground, seem to stare with almost a "frantic intensity" at a point between their own feet or over a strangers shoulder rather than run the risk of eye-contact (6).

At some point it is appropriate to list "the good points" about the Welsh as noted in a publication, *The Description of Wales* published in the 12th century and noted by John Winterson Richards (6).

1. Their respect for family
2. Their skill and courage in war.
3. Their love of choral singing and of poetry.
4. Their devotion to the Christian faith
5. Their hospitality and generosity
6. Their sense of humor.
7. Their natural acumen and shrewdness (they are more quick-witted than any other Western people).
8. Their great boldness in speaking and great confidence in response no matter what the circumstances (even in the presence of their princes—unlike the deferential English).

Some less good points have also been noted (6).

1. Their inconsistency and inability to keep their word. This is why the verb "to welsh" (meaning to go back on one's word) has entered into the English language.

2. Their tendency at one time to loot anything from anybody. Cattle raiding along the English border was popular at one time. Welsh poets wrote epics on the subject and the English also commemorated it in verse, but in a different tone:

> Taffy was a Welshman;
> Taffy was a thief;
> Taffy came to my house—and stole a
> leg of beef.

3. The Welsh are known to be stubborn. They prefer to call themselves "tenacious." An earlier author, Gerald, noted that the Welsh, even if defeated in battle, would come out ready to fight the next day as if nothing had happened. "They are very difficult to defeat in a long war," he observed. Many Welshmen are still fighting the one the English thought they won seven hundred years ago in 1295.

4. The Welsh may also excel at being excessive. Gerald has said, "You may never find anyone worse than a bad Welshman or anyone better than a good one."

5. Many have been visionaries such as the pirate Sir Henry Morgan who rose to deputy governor of Jamaica and became known as a very successful Welsh entrepreneur.

It has also been said, tongue in cheek, that the English ancestors who came from Northwest Europe's cold climate has given them cold personalities, whereas the Celtic Welsh with darker coloring, natural warmth of personality, music in their souls, and sometimes "hot tempered," must have come from warmer Mediterranean climes.

The Welsh people have had a great respect for religion. Their independent nature has led them strongly to the realm of non-conformism. The chapels were the most powerful forces for cohesion in Wales. There were often division and argument within the chapel causing a split in the congregation. One illustration was about how Mr. and Mrs. Jones leave the chapel for theological differences. "When the preacher visits them later to persuade them to come back, Mr. Jones says he cannot speak for his wife because they have since had theological differences with each other and worship in different corners of the room" (6).

Although this attitude may have cost the chapels the position of moral leadership they once had, the non-conformists have left a powerful legacy in the church history of the Methodists, Baptists, Congregationalists, Quakers, and others.

As discussed elsewhere, music has been the prime element of Welsh culture and it exists today in many forms: hymns in the chapels and at one time in the voices of workers as they leave the mine in a blackened condition; male choruses; operas; soloists; and the music of the harp and strings. So it is said the Welsh like their singing, more singing and even more singing!

Wales, with less than two million people, is a very small percentage of the population of the British Isles. Nevertheless, the Welsh have more than their share of names in the world history of academics, politics, music and the ministry.

The first alphabetical encyclopedia in English was published by John Harris, a clergyman, in 1704. Ephraim Chambers published his Cyclopedia in 1728 and at the time of his death, had collected and arranged additional materials. Dr. (Sir) John Hill, a botanist, published those materials and a section on botany as a supplement.

Dr. Abraham Rees (1743–1825), a Welsh Nonconformist

minister, published a revised and enlarged edition including the supplement and some 4,400 new items. Four hundred and eighteen copies were made between 1778 and 1788. Dr. Rees's work is known as the forerunner of *The Encyclopedia Britannica*. (58)

Another source lists Dr. Rees as a Presbyterian minister and president of the Presbyterian Board of London in the 18th century. Two grandsons of Dr. Rees came to America, both named William Rees. One came in 1832 with his wife and seven children as an ironworker. They came to Philadelphia and then to Pittsburgh where an "e" was added to the name. The other William Rees settled in West Turin, Lewis County in Northern New York. A third cousin was Samual Rees, who at the age of 19 began tutoring the sons of English noblemen in mathematics and natural philosophy.

Continuing with the Rees name in academia is another William Rees. Born in Aberysgir in 1887, the youngest of Daniel and Margaret Rees's eight children, William, at age five, moved with his family to Llanfrynach. The family had a small mill and farm. From here he attended local schools and in 1906, in his last year in Brecon County School, he won an "open exhibition" to the University College of South Wales. This was the beginning of his long and extra-ordinarily distinguished association with the learned institution, The University of Wales (30). In the 80th year of his most productive life, Dr. Rees, M.A., D.Sc, F.S.A., Professor Emeritus at the University of Wales (Fig. 9.1), was honored by the Brecknock Society of Breconshire

FIGURE 9.1
Dr. William Rees,
Professor Emeritus,
University of Wales

for his invaluable contributions to historical scholarship. His published works of medieval Welsh history can never be equaled.

Prince Edward, fourth child of Queen Elizabeth and Prince Philip and possibly fifth in line for the throne, was married around the turn of this century. His bride is Sophie Rhys-Jones. Others in the news with the Reese name include an actor, John Rhys-Davies, who played the dwarf, Gimli, in the *Lord of the Rings* films. He also appeared in *Indiana Jones and the Last Crusade* in 1989.

A dark unseen energy named "the cosmological constant" by Albert Einstein in 1917 is pushing the universe apart as he predicted, according to data collected in observations with the Hubble Space Telescope, led by Dr. Adam Reese ("Riess" in one account). Einstein's theories continue to be shown to be correct. Can his theory that time becomes light in eternity be proven?

Simon Rees, a London-based writer for *Military History*, continues his excellent research in his writing about Homer Lea, a frail American hunchback that helped make China a republic after World War I.

Charles Reese, long-time journalist with the *Detroit News* and now columnist for *King Features Syndicate,* is semi-retired, living in Orlando, Florida.

Several authors with the Rees name, writing on Welsh history, are referenced in the text. Among them are the following: J. F. Rees, Principal of the University College of South Wales, author of *Studies in Welsh History;* John Rhys, M.A., Principal of Jesus College, Professor of Celtic at the University of Oxford and co-author of *The Welsh People;* Alwyn and Brinley Rees, authors of *Celtic Heritage;* William Rees, Professor at the University of Wales (p. 56) and author of *The Medieval Lordship of Brecon* and *South Wales and the March: 1284–1415;* and Nona Rees, author of *Dewi Sant,* published in Welsh and not available for use or reference.

There have been a number of persons famous in world history that were either born in Wales or were of Welsh descent. One of the most notable was Lloyd-George of Dwyfor (1863–1945), the British statesman who led his country to victory in World War I. Although born in Manchester where his father, William George, was a school headmaster, both parents were Welsh. His mother was the daughter of David Lloyd, a Baptist minister in Caernarvonshire. David Lloyd-George was England's Prime Minister from 1916 to 1922 (58).

Thomas Edward (T. E.) Lawrence (1888–1945) was born in Wales of a Leicestershire family and became a British explorer and scholar. He was educated at Jesus College at Oxford and after serving under General Edmund Allenby in the Middle East and with Amir Faisal in Arabia during World War I, wrote of his adventures in *The Seven Pillars of Wisdom.* T. E. Lawrence, known as Lawrence of Arabia, died in a motorcycle accident on April 10, 1945 (58).

Frank Lloyd Wright, born in June 1869 of Welsh parents in Richland Center, Wisconsin, studied civil engineering at the University of Wisconsin. During his lifetime he revolutionized the concepts of design and materials in the world of architecture. Wright chose the name "Taliesin" for his home in Arizona. Taliesin was a Welsh poet who wrote epics of early medieval heroes.

One of the world's great actors in the later part of the 20th century is Sir Anthony Hopkins. Born on New Year's Eve in 1937 near Port Talbot, Wales, Philip Anthony was the only child of Richard and Muriel Hopkins. As a young boy, unhappy in school, he began reading books, drawing, painting and playing the piano. He obtained a scholarship at Cardiff's College of Music and Drama and later auditioned for Laurence Olivier at the National Theatre. After meeting Richard Burton, a fellow Welshman, when he was 15, Anthony decided he could also become an actor.

Richard Burton, born Richard Jenkins in 1925 in Pontrhydfen, Wales, has been described as a dark, somber actor with a splendid speaking voice. He excelled in heavy dramatic roles. He appeared in Broadway theatre and a number of exceptional movies.

Catherine Zeta-Jones was born in 1970 in Mumbles, a fishing village near Swansea, Wales. Studies in the arts and dramatics were readily available in her hometown. She took dancing lessons at age 4 and put on shows for her teacher and her dentist. Living in London with a tutor at age 15, she won roles in ten musicals, including *Annie*. After the musicals and a few years on British TV, she came to Hollywood. She maintains a home in Wales.

Bob Hope, the popular comedian, has mentioned that his Welsh mother loved to sing and was an influence for him to be an actor.

10
THE MUSIC

FOR CENTURIES Wales has had a reputation as the home of robust male choirs, attractive female harpists and fascinating music festivals. The Celtic culture has always put a high value on vocal, largely choral, music. Composers, musicians, singers and poets held annual contests, called eisteddfods, as long ago as the 12th Century. In medieval times it was a tournament in which poets and musicians competed for a seat of honor in the households of noblemen—a highly prized position since poets depended on patronage for their livelihood (4). The historical record indicates the first genuinely regional tournament appears to have been held in 1176 at Lord Rhys ap Gruffydd's castle of stone and mortar in Cardigan although references exist to earlier gatherings.

Sir Rhys ap Thomas, like his ancestor, was a leading magnet

of power in early Tudor southwest Wales. Such late medieval chieftains were expected to display 'largesse' translatable as 'conspicuous consumption.' Sir Rhys was no exception. Humility was not a virtue in the ancient world. His most famous display of showing off was the lavish tournament held at his Carew Castle in 1506 to celebrate his election as Knight of the Garter (35). The celebration is detailed in another account; however, it included all the features of an eisteddfod including music on the Eve of St. George's Day.

In the late 18th century Edward Williams, whose bardic name was Iolo Morganwg, reinvented the eisteddfod as a modern festival. An early informal one took place in Carmarthen in 1819. The first Royal National Eisteddfod was held in 1861 and has since become Europe's largest festival of competitive music-making and poetry-writing, attracting over a hundred thousand visitors and many thousands of competitors. It is now held during the first week in August, alternately in North and South Wales.

What makes the gathering unique is that it takes place solely in Welsh. There is simultaneous translation for some events and there is music, dance, handicrafts, clothing, food and souvenirs. There is usually a sizable non-Welsh contingent including Americans fascinated by their own Welsh ancestry.

As noted earlier the Welsh have, for any reason or on any occasion, enjoyed what has been called "singing, more singing and still more singing." It was common to hear miners, on leaving the mines and seeing the light of day, break out singing hymns. They have said, "as a poor people, all we have is our voice—we sing alone and we sing in choirs." Following the Reformation, simple chapels were built throughout the countryside accommodating nonconformist groups for hymn singing and preaching.

Christianity has been known for centuries as a singing faith.

Some of the hymns we sing to Welsh tunes are:

Guide Me, O Thou Great Jehovah
Immortal, Invisible
Come, Thou Long Expected Jesus
Jesus, Lover of My Soul
O the Deep, Deep Love of Jesus
Hail the Day That Sees Him Rise
Our Father in Heaven
God, That Madest Earth and Heaven

The latter is sung to the tune of "All Through the Night," the best known of all the simple and sincere Welsh melodies. In this ever-popular song, the poet delights in the peaceful contemplation of the stars. He sings of night as another form of light and as an aspect of pure beauty. The origin of "All Through the Night" is unknown although the first printing of it with Welsh words and an English translation was in the 1784 collection *Musical and Poetical Relicks of the Welsh Bards.* Various English texts have been circulated, but the one with the widest currency begins, "Sleep, my child and peace attend thee all through the night."

Besides John and Charles Wesley, many were involved in the preaching and hymn writing of the Evangelical Awakening of the 18th century. No two names, however, are more significant than John Newton and William Cowper (pronounced "Cooper") who collaborated to produce the *Olney Hymnbook,* a collection of 348 influential hymns. Newton, once a drunken sailor with an unsurpassed adventurous background, and Cowper, with a tragic and pitiful life—both from families with spiritual vitality—brought us some of the most treasured hymns. John Newton's mother believed in two things: the power of prayer and the reformation of her son. God answered her prayer by working a miracle in the heart of her son, as noted by Mrs. Cowman in her *Springs in the Valley*. Of particular note is John Newton's *Amazing Grace* (Fig. 10.1), possibly the most sung hymn of all time.

"Amazing Grace, how sweet the
sound, that saved a wretch like me!"

FIGURE 10.1
John Newton's *Amazing Grace*
with fifth stanza by John P. Rees

The hymn is also a basic tune of bagpipers. Tour buses crossing the border from England to Scotland will often be greeted by a piper playing *Amazing Grace*. Extra lines have been added to John Newton's four verses during the 19th century, however the best known of these is the fifth stanza as printed in *The*

Cokesbury Hymnal in 1923 and now always included. William J. Reynolds traced its origin to John P. Rees who printed the lines as a separate text in the second appendix of the 1859 edition of *The Sacred Harp*. Then 51 years later, E. O. Excell, *Coronation Hymns* (Chicago: 1910) added the stanza to Newton's hymn. *Amazing Grace* was then reprinted in Excell's form in the *New Evangel* (Dallas, 1911) and universally since that time.

A hymn of particular interest from the early 20th century and appearing in a Methodist hymnal under the category of Hymns of Integrity, is entitled *Rhys* (pronounced "Rice") (Fig. 10.2). Written by Rhys Thomas around the turn of the century, it is an admonition to himself of the noble values of the Christian life. The hymn is taken from Samuel Longfellow's *Hymns of the Spirit*, 1864, prepared in collaboration with Samuel Johnson.

FIGURE 10.2
Rhys Thomas' *Rhys*
Courtesy, Dr. John L. Wilson, Director of Music Ministries
Coral Ridge Presbyterian Church, Fort Lauderdale, Florida

Rhys Thomas was born in Wales, February 21, 1867, and died in London, October 16, 1932. He was educated at Cardiff, Wales and in London, and while still a comparatively young man, went to Winnipeg, Canada, where for twenty-eight years he was active in the musical life of that city and as an adjudicator at Canadian musical festivals. Prominent as a chorus conductor, choirmaster, and baritone soloist at Knox Church in Winnipeg, he composed many anthems, hymn tunes, and part songs. From 1925 he made his home in London.

In our time and in our own family, the grandson of True L. Reese, cousin Jim Reese, has displayed musical talent in several forms. Early lessons on the piano led to exposure of his singing talent, which he was able to use throughout his school years.

Prior to receiving a BA degree from Bryan College, Jim studied voice for four years under Gerald L. Woughter, a graduate of the famed Westminster Choir College. Here also he studied Harmony and Composition under such distinguished professors as David H. Heydenburk. Among the songs Jim has composed (words and music) are: *I Never Knew, Led By Love,* and *Bloom Where You're Planted (Fig. 10.3).*

Jim, also an accomplished trombone soloist and song leader, received his Bachelor of Divinity degree from Grand Rapids Baptist Seminary and has pastored Baptist churches in Moline, Michigan, and Kitchener, Ontario, Canada. Among his many accomplishments he has made music and pastoral presentations on radio and television and also has a number of musical recordings to his credit. Jim served for several years as soloist and song leader with an evangelistic team in the United States and Canada. At the time of this writing in 2005, Jim is semi-retired.

The Welsh harp tradition dates back over a thousand years and since that time, this special musical instrument has been the national instrument of Wales. The harp first became known in ancient times when King Saul (c. 900 B.C.) would experience a distressing spirit from God.

> And so it was—whenever the spirit from God was upon Saul, that David would take a harp and play it with his hand. Then Saul would become refreshed and well and the distressing spirit would depart from him (1 Samuel 16:23) (23).

Following the Welsh tradition in our time is the renowned artist and craftsman, William Rees. William has taught and played professionally since 1970 and is an accomplished multi-instrumentalist who has performed for audiences large and small. This early experience has given him a distinct advantage in understanding and building an instrument possessing qualities satisfying to the most articulate musician as well as the most discerning audience.

William Rees Instruments, LLC has been building custom and special order instruments for over thirty years. William and his sons, Garen and Bryant, now specialize in traditional (Fig. 10.4) and double harps. The beauty of wood and the art and science of woodworking find unified expression in every Rees instrument and flow from William's classical lutherie background.

The William Rees Instruments

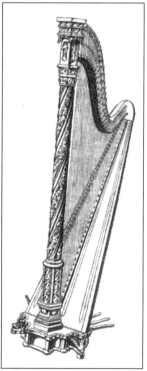

FIGURE 10.4
Harp by William Rees Instruments, LLC

FIGURE 10.3
Jim Reese's *Bloom Where You're Planted*
and album *Lead Kindly Light*

Chapter 10—The Music   69

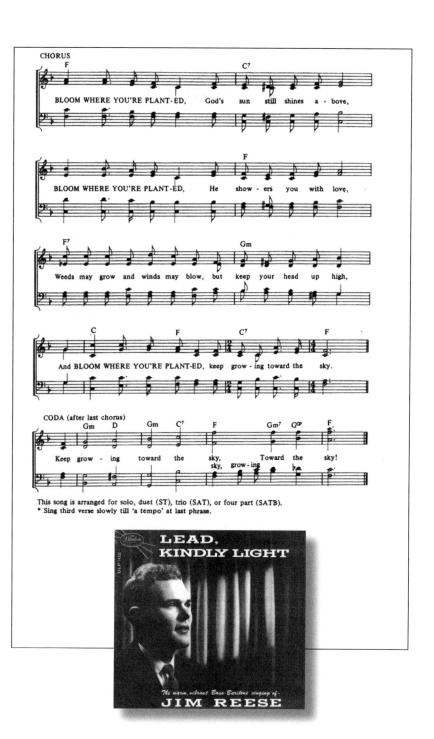

FIGURE 10.5
Linda Rice, harpist

lutherie and harp gallery is located at Harps on Main, Rising Sun, Indiana.

Linda Rice (Fig. 10.5), a present day harpist of note, has a surname derived from Rhys. Linda is the only female gospel harpist in the world and has a full-time touring schedule. It is said Linda's life stories and music can generate both laughter and tears. She plays a French Comac electric harp.

Welsh musician Richard Ormrod is a celebrated pianist who began studying piano at age 5. At age 10 he played with the Glamorgan Orchestra in Wales. He has won prizes in Rubenstein, MaKamichi and Leeds international competitions.

Another piano star of the 20th century is Rodger Williams, who with his Welsh name and musical talent, became the biggest selling pianist in the history of phonograph records. His fantastic keyboard virtuosity and sincere understanding of the music he plays has brought worldwide attention and admiration.

In addition to these and many other great instrumentalists of the Welsh-Celtic tradition there are the vocalists of the even greater Welsh singing experience.

An award winning singer/songwriter appearing on cruise ship entertainment programs is Mark Newsome, introduced as "from Wales—the land of song." Mark has starred in *Les Miserables* and has performed for English royalty. His maternal surname was Thomas.

The most notable of Welsh singers at the recent turn of the century is Charlotte Church (Fig. 10.6). At age 15, this classically trained prodigy was an internationally renowned vocalist and one of the top ten best-selling artists. Charlotte is known for her beautiful voice with an angelic sound. She has recently appeared in the United States with Julie Andrews and Christopher Plummer in *A Royal Christmas* with The Royal Philharmonic Concert Orchestra and other ballet and dance groups. Charlotte lives in Wales with her parents, and as a teenager, travels with them.

FIGURE 10.6
Charlotte Church

It is easy to become a lover of Welsh music when you hear the clear voice of a young artist sing, *I Want to Teach the World to Sing*. There are, no doubt, many other popular singers with Welsh ancestry. One may be Nora Jones, who recently won eight Grammy awards.

11
CHRISTIANITY

AS A MATTER of background, it seems appropriate to look at the nature of the Celtic pagan religion, the Celtic Christianity, the roles of St. David and St. Patrick, and the Reformation in general, as well as the English acceptance of Protestantism and the non-conformist approach of the Welsh.

The Celts were known to have thousands of gods who were spirits in the natural world—the sea, sky, stars, wells, mountains, and even individual trees with varying local names. All natural things surrounding the Celts were sacred. Their gods "talked" only to the Druids, the priestly caste, making known their great appetite for sacrifices of animals, humans, and precious objects. This gave the Druids great power because nothing could be accomplished without appeasing the gods by way of the sacred and secret rituals.

To protect their power they had no written language. All knowledge was committed to memory, requiring 20 years of learning to become a Druid. They claimed to be the source of all contemporary knowledge. They were the center of privileged activities even as "bards" reciting poetry, telling stories, singing praise to the chieftains and warriors, etc. (28). The Druid sanctuaries were in natural settings such as caves and forests. Auglesey seemed to be the center of the Druidic religion in Britain. They believed in the transmigration of souls, instilling in every warrior the belief that when he died he would be born again in another body. So, in battle they had no fear of death, making them recklessly brave. The Romans, normally sympathetic to tribal religions, went out of their way to destroy the Druids.

Prior to Dewi Sant there was another historic Celtic personality who is also recognized to this day. He is Saint Patrick, born at Bannavem in the northwestern part of England in A.D. 389. His father was a magistrate and a pastor of the British Church. Patrick describes himself as a willful and rebellious youth (43).

As a youth, he lived near the beach and one day at age 16, he and two of his friends spent the day in the breakers of the Irish Sea. They were sitting in the mouth of a cave by the beach planning their escapades for the next day when suddenly they saw a band of "Freebooters" (Irish pirates). The pirates came walking toward the cave. The boys leaped to their feet and ran, as Patrick describes it in his writings *Confession: Letter to Coroticus*. The boys ran into the rest of the pirates coming from the opposite direction. They were bound hand and foot and dragged aboard the pirate ship where there were several more English boys and girls.

They were taken to Hibernia and forced at whip point to march 200 miles inland, north of what is now Belfast, where they were sold into slavery. Patrick was sold to King Miliusc, a fierce Druid chieftain who had little concern for life. With little to wear, Patrick was sent out to care for the flocks and pigs. His companions were taken away but he had two others who never left him throughout the six years he was in slavery. He withstood the cold and gnawing hunger and endured the most miserable form of servitude (43) (58).

Patrick remembered what his father had said to him, "Patrick, there is a God who is able to deliver you. Do not forget that." He remembered hearing his father talk about how God had loved the world and had sent His only Son, way over on the other side of the world, to die there on the cross. He died for sins not His own, but for our sins.

In his *Confession,* Patrick tells how God opened his blinded eyes and gave enlightenment to his confused mind. He saw and understood and he committed his life to Jesus Christ as Lord, Savior and Master of all. In those several years he had left of servitude, he made a tremendous impact on those he met. They thought of him as that "holy youth."

After six years, in the middle of the night, he had a dream. He heard a voice that said, "Behold, your ship is ready." He left the swine and staggered through 200 miles of frigid forest finally coming to the beach. There was a ship of Irish Wolfhounds being taken for sale in Europe (43). Patrick found the captain and told him he had been kidnapped as a youth and made a slave in Ireland. He begged for transportation home, but was rebuffed and turned away. Patrick walked up the beach near the forest when a hand clasped his shoulder from behind and turned him around. A voice said, "Come back, boy, the captain changed his mind."

The author of the sermon *Who Really Was St. Patrick?,* Dr. D. James Kennedy adds, "Ah, when the Lord makes passage for you on a ship, the captain doesn't cancel the ticket" (43). Patrick went with the ship to Gaul, then back to his family in England.

Later, as a rugged young man, he tried to put his terrible experience out of his mind. Instead, the people of Ireland kept coming back to his mind. Some twenty years later he had another dream where he saw a whole host of Irish Druids standing on the beach looking out across the sea saying, "We beseech the holy youth to come and walk once more among us." Patrick took that to be the call of God upon his life.

His years near home in western England, Scotland and Wales, among his own Celtic people as well as their Druids, no doubt, helped prepare him for God's call. He set sail across the sea and landed at what is now Downpatrick. Going to the centers of power he began.to challenge the Druid chieftains, one after another. Finally, he went to Tara, the hill fortress of the High King of all the Druid chieftains, and there confronted him with the Gospel. For thirty years he crisscrossed Ireland (43).

The *Encyclopedia Britannica* states that Patrick personally converted and baptized 120,000 people. He built over 300 churches. He found Ireland totally pagan and left it resoundingly Christian.

In Thomas Cahill's book *How the Irish Saved Civilization (15)*, he states that right after the Huns and Vandals swept across Europe and destroyed all the books they could find, the Irish, converted by Patrick and his followers, took up "the great labor of copying all of Western Literature—all they could lay their hands on."

As for Patrick, every day his life was in mortal danger. Yet his accomplishments were absolutely gigantic. He was in the midst of some of the fiercest and cruelest people the world has ever seen. Patrick is buried in the churchyard of the Protestant Cathedral of Down in Downpatrick, Ireland. The gravesite marker is inscribed: "Patric" (43).

> Patrick in his "Lorica" (breastplate) says
> God's shield to protect me,
> From snares of devils,
> From temptations of vices,
> From everyone who shall wish me ill,
> Afar and near,
> Alone and in multitude.
> Christ to shield me today.

This saga of St. Patrick is included here to further indicate the pagan nature of the Celtic world in early Christian history. Whether England, Wales, Ireland, or Scotland, this was a world to itself in the Dark Ages, hundreds of years even before the Catholic Church had any measurable influence in the Celtic world.

The Romans had planted the roots of Christianity but the Celtic tribes tended to keep their old gods, even after the great accomplishments of Patrick. It took Irish "holy men" several centuries to adapt Christianity to Celtic tribal societies. After the 5th century A.D. they formed monastic centers. This was known as a dangerous time to be preaching Christian virtues but the early missionaries gradually won over chiefs by the example of their ascetic and disciplined lives. A few monks became known as "sancti," later translated as "saints." Hence, the Celtic saints caused the Dark Ages in Wales to become known as the Age of Saints. The substantial records of the Celtic saints notes their profound influence on early Welsh history. They built monasteries, hospices, and churches and became counselors of princes and were accredited with miraculous healing powers (28).

In *A Matter of Wales (10)*, author Jan Morris makes some fantastic observations in the chapter titled "A Holy Country," noting that the holiest Welsh place is Dewisland, Pebidiog, a stony protrusion from the coast of Dyfed. This was once the spiritual hub of the whole Celtic world, where their missionaries would come and go through the western seas on their way to evangelize pagan Europe. Everywhere there are the remains of shrines and chapels. Neither the Welsh nor the Normans ever fortified the peninsula in respect for its sacred meaning.

Some distance from the rocky shore of the wild Atlantic Sea, along the river Alun, stands the most venerated structure in all Wales, the cathedral of Dewi Sant, St. David, not only the Mother Church of Welsh Christianity but the pinnacle of all that is holy in Wales. It is the fourth holy building built since the original church was built by Dewi Sant in the sixth century (10).

Dewi Sant, now the patron saint of Wales, was known as an evangelist in his time and was reportedly canonized by the Church of Rome. By the sea in Dewisland is a ruined chapel on the site, we are told, where in about the year 500 his mother, St. Non, gave birth to him. In the Black Mountains, on the other side of Wales, is the site of his own first hermitage now occupied by an ancient church dedicated to him. Here Dewi Sant, barefoot, is pictured clad in skins, holding a stick he has cut from the woods, and a bell of miraculous powers. He lived the simplest of lives, drinking only water from the stream and became known as Dyfrwr, the Water Man. He ate wild leeks, which became the national emblem of Wales.

At Llanddewi Brefi is the churchyard where during an address to a great gathering of priests and people, the ground rose in a mound beneath his feet, elevating him above the crowd. Set into the wall of the church are two fragments of a stone, dated to the sixth century, which contain the earliest written reference of his existence (10).

At Tyddewi, where he established his own base after a lifetime of wandering, the saint ended his days. Supernatural signs foretold his death, according to a 12th century biographer. He tells of sorrowing crowds assembled in the little town to hear his last sermon which is considered the most famous of all the sermons preached in Wales.

"Lords, brethren and sisters," cried the old man, "rejoice and hold fast your faith and belief; and do the little things that you have heard from and seen in me." A great host of angels filled the town and all manner of delectable music was heard. The sun shone brightly "and Jesus Christ took unto Himself the soul of David the Saint with great pomp and honour." The date was March first, and on that day patriotic Welshmen still wear Dewi Sant leeks in their buttonholes to commemorate the national day of Wales (10).

The sites of early Celtic churches are often identified by place names beginning with the prefix "Llan" meaning an enclosure and a place where the Christians may bury their dead. There are churches in Wales where burials are confined to the south side, the north side being the devil's territory.

St. Illtud, the father of the Welsh Celtic saints, founded his monastery and school around A.D. 500 at Llantwit Major in the Val of Glamorgan, an area that had been well Romanized. The school has been called the first British University and was the seat of learning of the early Celtic church. St. David was a pupil as well as Gildas, an early writer. The school was continued until the arrival of the Normans.

St. Augustine was sent to England by Pope Gregory the Great in 597 to establish the See of Canterbury. He asked Celtic Welsh churches in 603 to join him in converting the pagan Anglo-Saxons. The Welsh declined, considering the Church of

Rome to be inferior to their own. They had no wish to be under Canterbury and their potential enemies, the Anglo-Saxons. The church in Wales thus became isolated from the rest of Christianity for up to two centuries, before finally submitting to Rome in A.D. 768. This ended the Celtic church but not Celtic religious art forms (28).

Poets became prominent in the Middle Ages, some embracing life in all its fullness, aware, as everyone was, that it is a brief and fragile thing. Many others dwelt upon the horrors of death and the tortures of hell. The Black Death (bubonic plague) was the greatest tragedy to strike Western Europe in historic times.

With the plague striking again and again in 1361 and 1369, periods of prosperity were intermittent. Taxes were heavy in order to fight the war with France. Since the conquest of Wales by Edward I in 1282 there were conflicts between Welsh laws and those the English imposed upon them (3).

All this took its toll on the church where there was intellectual fatigue and economic depression. The monks ceased to be the chroniclers of the history of their people. The Papacy became nothing more than another state, greedy for wealth and power. Its reputation suffered severely between 1379 and 1417 when there was one Pope in Rome and another at Avignon. A document in about 1380 notes that the 13 Cistercian monasteries of Wales had a total of only 71 monks.

The intellectual pre-eminence of the church was fading and becoming the subject of increased criticism. In Lola Goch's remarkable poem to the laborer, the poor man of the soil is portrayed as the only true Christian. These kinds of events made the acceptance of Protestantism by the Welsh a welcome change (3).

In England, however, the change was long and bloody. Prior to the union of Wales with England by Henry VIII in 1536, one of the most fundamental changes in the 16th century was the replacement of the nation's traditional Catholic belief with Protestantism.

Cardinal Wolsey, who became Henry VIII's Lord Chancellor in 1515, lost power when he was unable to secure Henry's divorce from Catherine of Aragon. He was charged with high treason but died enroute to prison in the Tower of London. The process began when it was evident the Cardinal's loyalty to the Catholic Church was greater than his loyalty to the king.

Sir Thomas More (1478–1535) succeeded Cardinal Wolsey as Chancellor and loyal servant of the king. More was one of Europe's foremost intellectuals, noted as a friend of Erasmus, Scholar of Rotterdam. However, he opposed Henry's divorce and break with Rome. He refused to take the Oath of Supremacy, acknowledging Henry VIII as head of the Church of England. He was sentenced to death for treason and was executed in the yard of the Tower in July 1535. Also, Bishop John Fisher (1469–1535), an intellectual who opposed Henry's divorce from Catherine and refused to recognize Henry as supreme head of the Church of England, was imprisoned in the Tower and executed for treason on June 22, 1535.

The king commanded that Bibles recently translated by Tyndale and Cloverdale into English should be displayed throughout the kingdom. English replaced Latin in church services. Monasteries were closed, leaving some 10,000 monks and nuns without a livelihood. Some became priests, others married nuns, some retired. Not all survived. Michael Whyting, 80, the last Abbot of Glastonbury, was dragged to the top of the Tower to be hanged, drawn, and quartered. Many, deeply traumatized by the closing, died as their sheltered lives ended.

Edward VI, Henry's son, encouraged the move to Protestantism, but next in line was Mary, his half-sister, known as "Bloody Mary." Her immediate order was for the restoration of Catholicism. Those opposing her were burned at the stake. Thousands of ordinary people died, creating long-lasting bitterness and anti-Catholic prejudice.

Elizabeth (1533–1603) inherited a confused and demoralized kingdom in 1558. When her reign ended in 1603, the Church of England was finally and firmly Protestant. The change was not accomplished without a mighty theological tussle as noted in "Life in Tudor England" (34).

The Puritans considered religious reform insufficient. Some Jesuit priests continued to practice in secret. The rituals of incense, candles, and monastic chants gave way to plain songs and tedious sermons, which were not to everyone's liking, and congregations began to decline. Thus, the Puritan movement was started in England.

The battle now began between the Welsh people's choice of religion and the religion of those seeking to impose their authority on them. It continued down the centuries in one form or another, helping to mold the character of Wales. Only four years separated the rupture with Rome by King Henry VIII and the forcible incorporation of Wales into his United Kingdom.

The Roman Church by then was stagnant in Wales, its bishops absent, its monasteries long past their prime, and so few priests. The exception was the most Catholic corner of Gwent by the English border with its long tradition of sanctuary. The differences were real between the Somersets of Raglan Castle with the nearby Jesuit cell of Cwm and a fanatical Protestant member of Parliament, who liked to search out Jesuits with an armed posse of his own servants (10).

Reformers prior to Martin Luther followed the arguments of

the Apostle Paul that the "revealed Word of God, the Bible, was the ultimate authority for all things spiritual." Paul's letter to the Romans planted the seed contributing to the formation of the Christian church and also played its part in bringing about the Protestant Reformation (1).

Authors Bell and Sumner, in their book *The Reformation and Protestantism,* provides a fascinating look at the beginnings of Protestantism. They refer to John Wycliffe as "the Morning Star of the Reformation." Wycliffe (1320–1384) was educated at Oxford and received a Doctor of Theology degree in 1372. He became a teacher of philosophy while also serving as a priest. His beliefs were similar to those of Luther, John Calvin, and other reformers (1).

Before Wycliffe there was Peter Waldo, the rich merchant of Lyons who chose poverty. His followers were known as Waldensians or the "Poor Men of Lyons." Some eighty of them were burned as heretics in Strasbourg in 1211 (1).

After Wycliffe's death in 1384, his followers became known as "Lollards." They were well organized and saw the scriptures as the cornerstone of their faith. They also condemned transubstantiation, the doctrine of purgatory, indulgences, and other aspects of the Catholic religion. They taught the importance of moral, upright living on the part of the clergy, so lacking in the popes of the Middle Ages.

A famous preacher of the "new faith" of the Lollards was the learned "Holy Rhys" of around 1390. His son, Ienan, was expelled from Margam Monastery for holding the opinions of his parents. Also, his grandson was imprisoned by Sir Matthew Cradoe for being of the "new faith" (37).

The bard and prophet, Thomas Llewelyn, was the first preacher to congregations of dissenters in Wales. Cleydon of

London was "burnt" (burned at the stake) for possessing a copy of the highly prized Lollard book known as the "Lanthorn of Light." The Lollards swarmed into Wales where, in the Black Mountains, "Oldcastle" hid for four years after escaping from the Tower.

It is claimed that the first Baptist church in Wales, after the Reformation, was formed at Ilston, near Swansea in 1644. However, Howell Vaughan, a Baptist, is known to have preached at Olchon in 1633. The first Welsh Baptist Association was organized in 1651. A rich history surrounds the Baptist church and its heroic Welsh leaders in the centuries following the Reformation.

John Miles is first mentioned in February 1649 in an act of Parliament for the better propagation of the Gospel in Wales. He left the clergy of the State Church to become a Baptist leader and formed the first Strict Communion Baptist Church in Wales. Miles is named with Vavasor Powell, Jenkin Jones, Hugh Evans, and twenty-two others as "approvers" to superintend preaching in the principality. Powell, Jones, and Evans formed the Open Communion Baptist Churches in Wales (37).

Vavasor Powell, born in 1617 of one of the best families in Wales, became one of the strongest characters of his age. He graduated from Jesus College, Oxford, and entered the Established Church as a curate to his uncle in Shropshire. One day a Puritan "reproved" him for breaking the Sabbath by taking part in sports. This occasion led to his conversion, after two years of mental agony for his sins.

In 1641 he began to preach the Gospel in earnest, but his life was threatened, so he fled to London in 1642 and joined the Parliamentary Army as chaplain. He preached two years in Kent, received a certificate from the Assembly of Devines as an accredited preacher and returned to Wales. He was immersed and became a Baptist in 1656.

As an itinerant preacher, Vavasor Powell was paid L66 10s (present day: about $100) per annum by the "Committee for Plundered Ministers." As for learning, energy, and success, he excelled in them all. He was constantly in the pulpit and the saddle, preaching two or three times a day in different places, and riding more than one hundred miles a week. It is said that by 1660 he had formed twenty-two churches in Wales and had twenty thousand followers. No man fired the hatred of the church party as he did. Once he denounced Oliver Cromwell from the pulpit at Blackfiriars (37). Powell suffered every kind of persecution for preaching, spent eight years in thirteen prisons, and died in the Fleet, a debtors prison.

Jenkin Jones, commonly called "the captain," was another grand example of this early Welsh independence and suffering for Christ. He was a gentleman of property and education, who had been in the army of the Commonwealth. He often appeared with the sword in one hand and the Bible in the other. His presence and address were majestic. Once when going to preach in Monmouthshire, a soldier of the Royal Army waylaid him, to kill him, but was so struck by his comeliness and bearing that his heart failed. He heard him preach and was converted (37).

The Church Party berated him as a "violent Anabaptist." It is known that his estates were confiscated and he was imprisoned at Carmarthen (37).

From the ascent of Charles II on May 29, 1660, no more was heard of the Association of Baptist Churches for 28 years. Persecution raged furiously against all Non-conformists in Wales and the Baptists, as usual, became the special subjects of hate, storm, and chains. The king's wrath burst upon the Non-conformists leading to the most iniquitous ordinances that despotism could desire. Under one pretense or another, butchery held high carnival for over a decade. Yet thousands would not bow the knee and among them some of the noblest Baptists Wales ever produced.

During this hot persecution, a petition from Carmarthen was sent to the king. It said,

> We dare not walk the streets and are abused even in our own houses. If we pray to God with our families, we are threatened to be hung. Some of us are stoned almost to death, and others imprisoned for worshipping God according to the dictates of our consciences and the rule of His Word.

The king, with characteristic heartlessness, sent them a polite answer with promises but paid no more attention. Sufferings increased day by day.

The authors of *The History of the Baptists* present an interesting review of the many aspects of establishing a church in the face of a government that wishes to control the church. Excommunication carried with it the denial of burial in the parish churchyards. The Baptists and others found it necessary to bury their dead in their own gardens, or where they could—often in secret and at night (37).

The Welsh Baptists found relief in The Toleration Act of 1689, protecting them in their worship and allowing them to leave their worship locations in the rocks and other hiding places.

There were many outstanding Welsh preachers during the centuries after the Reformation. There also were many warm controversies and sometimes debates on doctrinal subjects such as infant baptism, Arminianism, atonement, redemption, and others. They attracted strong opinion. Following are some of the leaders in Welsh Baptist history.

Joshua Thomas is celebrated as the leading historian. He was born in 1719. He walked thirteen miles to Leominster to worship with the Baptists every other Sunday. He was baptized in 1740 and began his ministry in 1746 at Leominster, where he remained for fifty years. He wrote *A History of the Welsh Baptists* and *A History of the Baptist Association of Wales.*

William Williams (1732–1799), born of wealthy Episcopalian parents and orphaned at age six, became Justice of the Peace and Deputy Lieutenant of the counties of Cardigan and Pembroke. William was educated in the best manner under trustees. He married young but lost his wife and was led to Christ by this tragedy. He entered the ministry and built a "commodious" chapel in Cardigan and filled it with devout hearers.

Mr. Williams was a part of the higher class of society and for a long period of time was Chairman of the Quarter Sessions. When he died, his loss as a magistrate was mourned "as a national" loss (37).

Morgan John Rhys (1760–1804) was the Welsh Baptist hero of religious liberty. After his baptism at Hengoed, he went to the Bristol Academy and entered the ministry in 1787. Prior to going to Bristol he established night schools and Sunday schools, far and near, in chapels, barns, and other places; supplying books and teaching the pupils himself without charge. Upon becoming a pastor, he aroused the denomination to the need for Sunday schools. Another of his many endeavors was a magazine *Cylchgrawn* which eulogized the American Constitution and demanded that religious support in Wales should be patterned after that in the United States. Spies were put on his trail. His landlord misled an arresting officer that came for him from London. Rhys was told by the landlord that he had better head for Liverpool. He left for the United States from there and was welcomed in

Philadelphia by Dr. Rogers (37).

Joseph Harris, pastor at Swansea, was born in 1773. So great was his thirst for knowledge that he became one of the chief men of letters in the nation and wielded great influence. He became a controversial theologian by his writing in various pamphlets and his work, *The Proper Divinity of Our Lord Jesus Christ,* published in 1816. Bishop Burgess and other English clergy pronounced "high eulogies" on the book.

Mr. Harris published a Welsh weekly magazine in 1814, *Star of Gomer,* which became a great success as a monthly in 1818 with broad and thorough discussions. This earned him the title of "Father of Welsh Journalism." He also published a Welsh and English Bible and a hymnbook for his Baptist denomination (37).

Christmas Evans (Fig. 11.1), the prince of Welsh preachers, was born on Christmas Day in 1766 and was named after that holiday. His father was very poor and died when Christmas was about nine years of age. Mourning his own ignorance, he resolved to learn. At eighteen he was converted and united with the Arminian Presbyterians. He memorized a sermon of Bishop Beveridge and one of Mr. Roland's and delivered them in a wonderful manner.

Needing a means to support his hopes, he left for England to work in a harvest field. He soon fell into the hands of a mob and received a blow that left him insensible and his right eye blind for life. Being aroused to new diligence he was immersed on his faith in Christ in the River Duar by Rev. Timothy Thomas and united with the Baptist Church at Aberduar.

At age 22, Christmas was ordained at Lleyn as the pastor of five small Baptist churches. Frequently he walked twenty miles and preached four or five times on a Sabbath with marked results. He was captivated by the preaching of Robert Roberts, a hunch-backed Calvinistic Methodist of marked eccentricities. In a short time Christmas Evans portrayed remarkable preaching powers. He traveled on foot through towns and villages where crowds gathered in chapels, burying grounds or harvest fields to hear him as his fame spread (37).

FIGURE 11.1
Christmas Evans

At a meeting of the Association on a hot day in 1794 Evans was the third speaker. Soon people began to weep and praise God and clap their hands for joy far into the night. Many were saying "the one-eyed man of Anglesea is a prophet sent from God." In his lifetime he had preached one hundred and sixty-three times before the Association. He was in the front rank in the Welsh ministry for over fifty years.

Much is said about Christmas Evans in the reference *History of the Baptists* which might proclaim him to be one of the greatest preachers of all times. His most famous sermon, "The Demoniac of Gadara," was heard by most every Welshman in his day. He acted out the part of a fiend that lived in rocks and slept in tombs with the dead. In lucid moments he was gentle, then roared like a lion, howled like a wolf, and raved like a tiger. He was the terror of Gadara until Jesus came, restored the tortured mind, and filled the land with joy. The sermon held throngs spellbound for as long as three hours.

Just before Christmas passed from this life at Swansea on July 19, 1838 he said, "I am leaving you. I have labored in the sanctuary fifty-three years and this is my comfort—that I have never labored without blood in the basin." With his last breath he referred to a verse in an old Welsh hymn, then waved his hand as if with Elijah in the chariot of fire and cried, "Wheel about, coachman; drive on!"

John Jenkins was also an outstanding self-educated minister born into a poor family in 1779. At age 14 he found one of John Rhees' (Morgan John Rhys) evening schoolbooks and learned to read the Welsh Bible. He was baptized at Llanwenarth and became a pastor at age 21. He built a strong church and became a leading writer in the denomination. In 1811 he published a body of divinity entitled *Silver Palace* and followed it in 1831 by a commentary of the Bible. Lewisbury University conferred upon him the degree of Doctor of Divinity in 1852.

Timothy Thomas (1754–1840) of Aberduar, was a most robust servant of Christ. He was the son of the "Thunderer" of the same name. After his ordination he went everywhere preaching the Word. He baptized about 2,000 converts, among them, Christmas Evans.

John Williams (1806–1856) was the thorough scholar and translator of the New Testament into modern Welsh. At age 20, without a master, he had acquired a good knowledge of English and Latin and considerable progress was made in Greek, Hebrew and mathematics. At 21 he published an English grammar in Welsh and English. He was ordained a home missionary among the Baptists in 1834.

Williams devoted himself to the translation of the New Testament and finished the task in four years. Although nobody pretended that his choice of words were unfaithful, the cry was raised that he had made a "Baptist Bible." He suffered the greatest possible abuse, as if he were a God-fearing criminal. Wales produced few harder workers or more diligent inquirers after the truth. The coarse abuse of men wounded his loyal soul. John Williams' health sank, and he died at age 50.

Thomas Rhys Davies was known as a character and as "Old Black Cap" because he wore a velvet cap in the pulpit. For years he stood second to Christmas Evans in popularity. He was a traveling preacher, and so great was his work that he said there were few rivers, brooks, or tanks in Wales in which he had not baptized.

During 47 years he preached 13,145 sermons, averaging over five per week and left a minute record of the time, place, and text of each sermon. Each sermon may have been preached as many as twenty times, but seemed to delight the people each time. It was said his sermons were so natural they seemed to have been born with him. Despite a slight impediment in his speech, there was a great mystery about his eloquence. He preached his last sermon near Swansea. He then said, "I am very ill. Let me die in the bed where Christmas Evans died." He fell asleep on Sunday and was buried in Evans' grave.

Robert Ellis (1812–1875) was a prodigy. Although with nine months training under John Williams as his only schooling, he excelled as an antiquarian, bard, lecturer, preacher, and Biblical interpreter. He was a gifted writer, authoring many poems and *Five Lectures on Baptism.* His greatest work was his *Commentary on the New Testament* in three volumes.

William Morgan, D.D., one of the most able ministers of North Wales, devoted his life to the interests of the Baptists of Holyhead from the year 1825. He was the first biographer of Christmas Evans and published three volumes of sermons. Georgetown College, Kentucky, honored him with the title Doctor of Divinity. After a very useful ministry, he died in 1873.

John Emlyn Jones, M.A., L.L.D. (1820–1873) was pastor of Baptist churches at Nebo, Cardiff, Merthyr Tydvil, and Llandudno. He was a very eloquent preacher and distinguished himself as an author in works of theology, history, and general literature. He also translated *Gill's Commentary* into Welsh. He was a poet of eminence, attaining the honor of Chair Bard, B.B.D. His Doctor's degree was conferred upon him by the University of Glasgow.

Hugh Jones, D.D. (1831–1883) was born at Anglesea of parents with musical talent. He was baptized at Llanfachreth at age fourteen and preached his first sermon at a weekly experience meeting. His first public sermon was preached in 1851 before he entered college at Haverfordwest in 1853. In 1859 Mr. Jones joined Dr. Pritchard as Associate Pastor at Llangollen. The Baptist College was established there in 1862 and the co-pastors were appointed co-tutors.

When Dr. Pritchard resigned in 1866, Dr. Jones became principal of the College, resigning his pastoral obligation. The institution saw great prosperity due to the dedication, keen intellect, strong will, and the hard work of Dr. Jones (37).

Hugh Jones' health failed for the second time in 1883 with fatal consequences. He left a widow and 11 children. The children became true orphans when their mother died two years later. In every respect Dr. Jones was a man of "rare mark." He left a deep impression on the Baptist interests of the principality. His profound biblical scholarships and thorough consecration to Christ are abundantly seen in his works *The Bible and Its Interpretation* and *The Act of Baptism.*

The list of Welsh Baptist leaders would continue as the church prospered around the turn of the century. It is also obvious there has been a great molding influence exerted upon the Baptist churches of the New World.

George Fox, born in Fenny Drayton, Leicestershire in 1624, is considered the founder of The Religious Society of Friends. From the time of his youth he thought deeply about religion. He walked around England, talking with priests and other authorities trying to find true religion. He found that men had an amazing amount of knowledge about the Christian faith, but little personal connection with God.

When his hopes in men were gone, he heard a voice that said, "There is one, even Christ Jesus, that can speak to thy condition," and then he exclaimed, "When I heard it, my heart did leap for joy." At age 23, George Fox began a traveling ministry encouraging seekers to hear and obey the voice of Christ within them. He was beaten, imprisoned, and bodily thrown out of some churches. He told a judge who had sentenced him for 'blasphemy' that he should tremble before God. The judge replied, "You folks are the tremblers, you are the Quakers!" The name stuck.

George Fox visited Wales three times after 1657. Quakerism took a strong hold in Radnorshire despite the incredible suffering caused by persecution. There were some 50,000 followers by 1660, eight years after Fox's vision on Pendle Hill in Northern England. A quarter of an acre was donated in 1673 for a burial ground. Around 1717 a building was built nearby called "The Pales," (Fig. 11.2) for meetings. Many immigrated to America in the ensuing years.

FIGURE 11.2
Scratchboard illustration of The Pales

From about 1570 Puritanism, as inspired by John Calvin's vision of the early church, was a serious challenge to the Elizabethan Religious Settlement. Calvin's followers wished to transform the Church of England into a Presbyterian Church. They demanded a bishopless church of intense moral consciousness such as John Knox was promoting in Scotland (3).

During the reign of Elizabeth, the Puritan representing the Welsh constituency was Edward Downlee, a member of Parliament for Carmarthen. Downlee presented to Parliament a treatise which pleaded for preachers to expound the gospel to the Welsh. John Penry, a native of Breconshire who had embraced Presbyterianism while a student at Cambridge, wrote the treatise. Penry was vicious, in two other treatises, in his condemnation of the Welsh clergy and bishops of Wales. He was sentenced to death and was hung May 19, 1593. Although Presbyterians gained a foothold in Flintshire, they remained a minority in Wales (3).

Even though Luther's ideas were winning considerable support in populous areas of England, followers were few in Wales. One, Thomas Capper, was burned for criticism of Henry VIII's church policy. His life was ended at Cardiff in 1542.

Griffith Jones (1683–1771) was a farmer's son from the fertile Teifi Valley. In his youth he had a religious experience so intense that he was overwhelmed with a desire to save souls. His career was strongly influenced by Sir. John Philipps. The support of the Squire of Picton Castle was crucial to Griffith Jones. He became a highly talented preacher, sometimes angering the ecclesiastical authorities when his fellow clerics complained of his custom of visiting their parishes and arousing the emotions of large congregations (3).

Realizing that sermons did not always suffice, Jones had the single-mindedness and energy to do what many had suggested was most needed: circulating schools. By the middle of the 18th century Wales was one of few countries with a literate majority. "The purpose of this spiritual charity," he wrote, "is not to make gentlemen, but Christians and heirs to eternal life." The interesting history of Griffith Jones and his schools intertwined with the Methodist Revival. The region where the schools were most numerous was the cradle of the revival and Griffith Jones was a friend and spiritual father to its leaders.

Traditionally, the beginning of revival is dated to Whit Sunday 1735, when Howel Harris experienced a religious conversion at Talgarth, Breconshire (3). Harris began to evangelize among the inhabitants of the enchanting villages around Llangors Lake and in 1737 he met Daniel Rowland who was similarly occupied in the Aeron Valley. Both men were members of the clergy of the Established Church. By now revivals were afoot in England, Scotland, Germany, and North America for Methodism was part of a religious awakening experienced throughout the Protestant world (3).

There were close links between the Welsh Revivalists and the leaders of English Methodism, George Whitefield (pronounced "Whitfield") and John Wesley. It would be a mistake to believe, as some have, that the initial stimulus for the Welsh revival came from England. The message of the Revivalists was terrifyingly simple:—eternal torment in hell would be the fate of those who did not have a personal awareness of Christ's sufferings and sacrifice for their sins.

Howell Harris attracted large congregations and thousands came to hear Daniel Rowland. The excitement of a Methodist Meeting was more appealing than the formality of the parish church or even the gatherings of the Non-conformists. The Revivalists were talented artists, their meetings were theatre and their hymn singing was jubilant. William Williams, hymn writer and author of some 90 books and pamphlets, became a part of the Methodist revival with his volume of hymns (3).

In the early days Methodism was an interdenominational movement with Anglicans, Independents, and Baptists following the "Methodist Way." The Welsh Methodists looked to George Whitefield as their theological leader. His belief differed somewhat with that of John Wesley who visited Wales on almost fifty occasions. John Wesley was the father of the Wesleyan movement (3).

The Revivalists set a new tone for Non-conformists, Independents, Baptists, and others by featuring an eloquent sermon and the singing of hymns. Almost every author of Welsh history tries to cover some of the religious events, which strongly impacted most of the population in the centuries following the Reformation.

12
EMIGRANTS

DUE TO wars, persecution, and hardship, emigration became an event in the lives of many people in the last half of the 16th century and the first half of the 17th century. Much of the early movement of people was due to the fact that the Reformation brought great turmoil to some parts of Europe, England, Netherlands, northern France, and German provinices bordering the Holy Roman Empire.

Much light is shed on the difficulties of establishing a national religion in *The England and Holland of the Pilgrims,* by Henry and Morton Dexter (48), originally published in 1906. Dr. Henry Dexter died in 1890 leaving his great detailed study to be completed by his son, Morton. Some thoughts follow from this most interesting study of the times.

King Henry VIII died in 1547 leaving England's three million people heavily in debt. It became necessary to borrow money in Antwerp and devalue the coinage, all leading to serious problems in the area of religious development, after the removal of Catholicism.

Edward, born in 1537 and the son of King Henry and Jane Seymour became the child king, Edward VI, at age 10. The government, a Lord Protector, and the Privy Council, controlled him.

> Throughout his reign, public life was corrupt, and private life was alarmingly impure. Business was in a bad way. Laborers were driven to choose between starvation, stealing, or begging. A cow selling for six shillings could not now be bought for forty shillings. Even the jails were filled (48).

Edward VI reigned six years, dying in 1553 at age 16.

Mary, the next in line to the throne, was born in 1516 to King Henry and Spanish Catherine of Aragon. Queen Mary wed Philip II, King of Spain. They became joint monarchs of England, Spain, Ireland, Netherlands, Naples, and Jerusalem in 1553. Queen Mary I, noting the deplorable conditions and finding a popular welcome for Romanism, delivered a staggering blow to the Reform Movement. By November 1554 the House of Commons resumed the yoke of the Pope, by a vote of 360 to 1.

Mary forbade the marriage of clergy. More than 800 Reformers fled to the Continent, among them bishops, deans and some 50 Doctors of Divinity. Hundreds of noblemen, tradesmen, merchants, and craftsmen became refugees. She had some of the noblest men in England burned at the stake. More than 300 others suffered death and imprisonment due to persecution of Non-conformants.

Mary I became a wretched queen, brooding upon her misery until her death in 1558. King Philip, known as a bitter Romanist, had returned to Spain earlier, without further concern for Mary's expectation of bearing an heir to the throne (48).

Next in line to the throne was Elizabeth I, the daughter of Henry VIII and Anne Boleyn. She favored Protestantism and in her 50-year reign was able to stabilize England's problems with finances and religion. Wales, as a part of England since 1536, suffered in the same manner through the rest of the 16th century.

In 17th century Wales, most workers with limited educations could only find employment in the slate quarries, coal mines or in raising sheep. Many were barred from civil jobs, which were more often given to families of gentry or those with some education.

As Protestant leaders returned late in the 16th century, a few grammar schools were opened. The one Welsh (language) university was Jesus College, Oxford, open only to members of the Anglican Church. Traveling academies, known as "Locomotive Schools," started by clergyman Griffith Jones of Llanddowror in Dyfed, taught religious subjects in the Welsh language. His effort was credited with bringing literacy in the native language to many thousands before running out of funds (10).

Without an English education the Welsh were becoming isolated from the world. Until the Victorian Era they were putting up with a "rag-bag" of educational opportunities; some started by religious bodies, some simple "dame schools" teaching needlework and spinning and some put together by disabled or retired seamen (10). By 1820 the demand for schools was such that English was taught in a more modern school system and the loss of native talent was greatly reduced.

While the glory of England declined, the Netherland lowlands prospered. Until 1831, Netherlands included Belgium and Luxembourg. Antwerp was the world financial center and often dealt harshly with the "wasteful debtor nation of England."

On July 26, 1581 William I of Orange, in control of the Calvinist lands of the northern provinces of Netherlands, issued a declaration of independence (11).

For the many who were able, the political, religious, educational, and financial conditions of the times gave more than ample reason to leave England and Wales. In addition to both Catholic and Protestant refugees (including the Pilgrims and Quakers) emigrating from England and Wales to Ireland, Holland, and northern France (Brittany), there were many others looking for a better life in prosperous Netherlands.

And from there, facilitated by the large Dutch shipping empire, it became possible to go anywhere in the known world, including America.

Cymru—"Land of Fellow Countrymen"

The identifying icon for the following section, *Part IV—The Historical Rhys,* is the Red Dragon, another national symbol of Wales. It dominates the white and green background of the Welsh flag.

PART IV

The Historical Rhys

13

A ROOTS RESEARCH

IN THE preface to his *Annals and Antiquities of the Counties and County Families of Wales (51),* first published in London in 1872, author Dr. Thomas Nicholas has much to say of the Welsh gentry in response to the frequently expressed desire that a more complete and faithful account be provided of the great families of the Principality.

It is in this publication that we find a rather complete "visitation," as Dr. Nicholas says, of the public life of our most likely Welsh ancestor, Sir Rhys ap Thomas. By law a Welshman held rank and claimed property "by kin and descent." He must show lineage through nine generations. "A person past the ninth descent formed a new Pen Ceaedyl or head of family." Its elder represented every such family and he was delegated to its national council.

In this sense genealogy was a constituent of social and political life of the Cymry (Welsh) before the time of Howel the Good. Some families had their own "heraldic bards" and genealogists, who on state and ceremonial occasions, recited the descent of the lord of the house and recorded facts at births and marriages. Upon the death of an elder, the family bard pronounced his "eulogium," detailing his honorable descent and worthy actions.

Dr. Nicholas, after examining voluminous ancient documents from different quarters containing matters in common from early times and noting the great care that must have been taken, "sees no reason for questioning the reliability of Welsh pedigrees." Wales is a country of old annals, old customs, old families as well as old rocks, old mountains and old castles.

Again, the author of the *Annals* suggests that the aristocracy of Wales have an ancestry, which for antiquity and position need fear no comparison with others. A large number can trace back to before the Norman Conquest of 1066. Cruffydd ap Cynan, Rhys ap Tewdwr, and Llewelyn the Great are quite as historical names as Edward the Confessor, William the Conqueror, or Knut the Great.

The position of the gentry of Wales is of particular interest. In no country did great families in past ages hold to the general population a relation more nearly approaching the paternal and patriarchal. In feudal times, the lord and vassal in Wales, under the influence of the warmth, temperament and disposition to personal attachment and clanship, by which the Celt is marked, were more like co-partners in the family estate than servant and master. Many things change, but the temperament and tendencies of the Celtic race are immortal.

The tone of Dr. Nicholas' work and the extent of the work of Roots Research, Inc., in regard to the large number of generations covered from the 9th to the 15th centuries, would indicate data may be available to link our adventurous ancestor Andries Rees to Sir Rhys ap Thomas.

Although Roots Research is no longer in existence, its efforts can serve as a basis for further work. The University of Wales and the associated National Museum in Aberystwyth on the central west coast of Wales is reported to be an excellent source of Welsh historical data of all kinds.

The two ancestral lines are presented in a genealogical and historical sketch manuscript (45) that contains the Rhys name in preponderance. The first line includes a Sir Thomas Rhys after about 18 generations. The second line, although not as detailed, leads to Sir Rhys ap Thomas and his brother, Owen ap Thomas.

The first line begins with the King of Powys in A.D. 876 as king over most of Wales. He married Lady Angbarad, daughter of the King of Britons (not named). They had a son, Cadell, who became Prince of South Wales. Cadell married Lady Reingar, daughter of Tudor-Trevor, Earl of Haverford. Their son, Howell, became the King of Wales and was the father of Owen who in turn was the father of Einion. Einion married Lady Nesta, daughter of the Earl of Devonshire, and was the father of Tudor-Mawr who married Gwenlian. They had a son named Rhys. Rhys had issue by his wife, Lady Gwladys, daughter of the Prince of Powys, named Griffith. Griffith married another Lady Gwenlian, the daughter of Griffith ap Cynan, Prince of North Wales. Their son, also named Rhys, became Chief Justice of South Wales. This Rhys married a Lady Gwenlian, daughter of Macod, Lord of Bromfield. Their son, Rhys Gryd, Lord of Yestradtywy married Lady Joan, daughter of Richard de Clare,

Earl of Hertford. They were the parents of Rhys Mechyllt, who became the Lord of Llandovery Castles. Rhys Mechyllt died in the year 1242 leaving a son named Rhys Vaughn, who had issue by his wife, Lady Gladwys, daughter and heir of Griffeth, Lord of Cymcydmaen, named Rhys-Gloff, also Lord of Cymcydmaen. Rhys-Gloff married Lady Gwyril, daughter of Maclywn ap Cadwallader, and was the father of Madoc, Prince of Powys.

Prince Madoc was the father of Trahairn-Goch who was the father of David-Goch. David-Goch married Lady Mawd, daughter of David Lloyd and fathered Evan (Ievan). Evan was the ancestor of the Rhys (Rees) family of Dinefwr Castle from which was descended the branch of the family that went into England and then to America.

Sir David Rhys, lineal descendant of Lord Rhys of Dinefwr, married Gwenlian, the daughter of Griffith-Konan, King of Wales. They had a son, Sir Thomas Rhys. Sir Thomas Rhys married Mawd, daughter of Sir William de Brewys and had a son, Sir David. With his wife, Gladys, daughter of Redwallen, Prince of Powys, he fathered the Reverend David Rees of Southwark (London). He was the father of another Reverend David Rees of Cardigan, Wales. This Reverend David Rees married Mawd, daughter of Sir Meredith Owen of South Wales.

The second line begins with Urien Rheged, Prince of Rheged, Wales. (Rheged was a town in an area of Celtic people, around A.D. 700, in what is now Northwestern England.) Prince Rheged was the fifth in descent from Coel Codevog, a king of the Britons. Many communities with a significant population had their own king in the so-called Dark Ages after the Romans left the British Isles. Prince Rheged resided in Carmarthen, Wales when he married a daughter of Furlois, Duke of Cornwall. The Prince was the ancestor of Sir Elidir Ddu, who married a daughter of Sysyllt, Lord of Contreselfy, and fathered Philip. Philip was the father of Nicholas, who had a son named Griffith, who left issue of two sons: Thomas and Owen. Of these, Thomas was the father of Sir Rhys ap Thomas and Owen ap Thomas (45).

14
THE CASTLES IN RHYS HISTORY

WALES has the highest proportion of castles per unit of land of any country in the world. A castle may be defined as the private fortress of a king or nobleman and existed as a part of the feudal system. Castles bring to mind not only the defensive structures built to thwart an aggressor, but legends of King Arthur, medieval settings of romance, or of knights and ladies of royalty.

Celtic tribes may have built a number of the hilltop fortifications as early as 1000 B.C. These were wooden structures and no doubt served as points of resistance to the invading Romans before 50 B.C. The first true castles were built in the 11th century before the Norman Invasion of 1066. William the Conqueror, Duke of Normandy (William I of England), built motte and bailey type "castles" as a base from which the countryside could be pacified. Edward the Confessor, Saxon King of England (1042–1066), built some early Norman style castles in the troublesome borderlands or "Marches" between England and Wales before the Norman Invasion (39).

King Edward I of England built some 17 stone castles, some described as "magnificent and intimidating" after subduing Wales in 1295 and defeating Llywelyn the "Last." Llywelyn's father, Llywelyn the Great, had built a number of castles in Gwynedd and even beyond his territory. The castles built by Edward I extended across the north and midsection of Wales, mostly in the last half of the 13th century and were an attempt to dominate the uncooperative and fractious Welsh natives.

As may be seen today, many if not most of the castles built in the 11th to 14th centuries have been abandoned, slighted, or demolished. Some are even being used as sources of building stone. Several have been designated as historical sites. In all, including the Marches border areas, there were at least 88 castles in Wales.

Several Welsh castles, mostly in southern Wales (Fig. 14.14), appear in the history of Rhys families. As noted elsewhere, families with this surname commonly include the names Gruffudd, Owain (Owen), Dafydd (David), Llywelyn, Thomas, and others. In modern times most Welsh castle sites are owned by the government and some are listed as tourist attractions or of historical interest. The Rhys surname appears in the history of several castles beyond those mentioned here. An Anglo-Welsh churchman by the name of Gerald left a vivid picture of Welsh life in the

12th century in his *Journey through Wales*. His stories shed much light on the ancient castles (39). One tells of an interesting occasion regarding a Rhys family of Kidwelly.

The original wooden Kidwelly Castle was built by Roger, Bishop of Salisbury, in 1106 in Carmarthenshire. The site was well chosen as it could be supplied by sea and controlled the river along the steep ridge upon which it was built. The castle was rebuilt by Rhys ap Gruffudd in the years between 1190 and 1196. In the 13th century it was rebuilt in stone (Fig. 14.1) by the Norman family, de Chaworth, with domestic apartments and defensive refinements such as "murder holes" through which missiles and rocks could be poured upon unfortunate attackers. In his writings, Gerald relates how a countrywoman named Gwenllian played a major role in a drama near the castle in 1136. Gwenllian

FIGURE 14.1
Kidwelly Castle, Carmarthenshire

was the daughter of Gruffudd ap Cynan, King of Gwynedd, and the wife of Gruffudd ap Rhys, Lord of Deheubarth. Quoting Geraint Roberts (39),

> Gwenllian was no shrinking violet and showed that (Celtic) women could often attain prominent roles in Welsh society. During a time of trouble in the area Gruffudd, her husband, went to ask his father-in-law for reinforcements. Gwenllian raised an army in his absence and led them against a force led by Geoffrey, the Bishop's steward, and Maurice de Londres, a Norman, who was to become Lord of Kidwelly when Bishop Roger died.

Gerald said,

> Gwenllian was like Penthesilea, Queen of the Amazons. She had been so sure of victory that she brought two of her sons with her. One of them, Morgan, was killed and the other, Maelgwn, was captured. Gwenllian and many of her followers were beheaded on the battlefield, which is still known as Maes Gwenllian (Gwenllians Field) to this day.

Her husband succeeded in winning his lands back from the Normans but he died within the year. He had not been a particularly powerful ruler, but one of his and Gwenllian's sons, Rhys, was to make his mark upon the history of Wales. Rhys was only four or five years of age at the time of his mother's death but was eventually to become ruler of Dehebarth in his own right and to become known as "Yr. Arglwydd Rhys," the Lord Rhys. Kidwelly Castle would be a constant thorn in his side. Rhys and one of his sons, Rhys Grgy, both captured and held Kidwelly Castle on separate occasions, although both lost control after a time (39).

The last refinements were added to the castle by Sir Rhys ap Thomas (1449–1525) around the turn of the 16th century. This Lord Rhys became prominent as a supporter of Henry Tudor (Henry VII) who was born in Pembroke Castle (Fig. 14.2) in nearby Pembrokeshire.

The remains of one of two castles in Cardigan is understood to have been built by Rhys ap. Gruffudd, known as "Yr Arglwydd Rhys," the Lord Rhys, around 1170. He has been identified with the castle that is now inside the modern town (Fig. 14.3). It is believed that the Rhys castle in Cardigan was the first stone-built Welsh castle. Lord Rhys also built or held many castles including

Photo © Irma Hale

FIGURE 14.2
Pembroke Castle, Pembrokeshire

FIGURE 14.3 Photo © Paul Adams
Cardigan Castle *(remains, foreground)*, Cardigan, Ceredigion

those at Rhayader (no visible remains), Dinefwr (Fig. 14.13), and Cilgerran (p. 6).

Caernarfon Castle (Fig. 14.4) at water's edge in northwest Wales is one of the most impressive fortifications in the British Isles. It is a fantastic monument to the English conquest of Wales. It is also the anchor to a chain of castles built by Edward I to consolidate his conquest and ensure that the English maintain a stranglehold on the Welsh. The castles were expensive to erect (39).

On a tour in July 2002 we visited the Caernarfon Castle. In a corner of this massive structure is a museum of artifacts of the times and graphic presentations. The first to catch the author's eye was the story and picture as shown in the figure depicting the end times of Rhys ap Thomas (Fig. 14.5, lower right corner).

Dryslwyn Castle (Fig. 14.6) stands upon a prominent hill near a major crossing of the River Tywi, west of Llandeilo, Carmarthenshire. It was probably built prior to 1245 by one of

Chapter 14—The Castles in Rhys History   113

FIGURE 14.4
Caernarfon Castle, Gwynedd

Lord Rhys ap Gruffudd's descendants. In 1271 Maredudd ap Rhys of Deheubath died within its walls. The castle really came into prominence when Maredudd's son, Rhys ap Maredudd, rose in revolt against Edward I on June 8, 1287. Although Rhys and his father had supported the kings of England against the princes of Gwynedd he felt "hard done" by the royal Justiciar of West Wales and the constable of nearby Dinefwr Castle, a Rhys stronghold at another time (39).

Rhys soon found himself and defenders in Dryslwyn under siege with the army of 11,000 men of Edward,

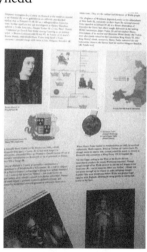

FIGURE 14.5
Caernarfon Castle display depicting Wars of the Roses events, demise of King Richard III, rise of the Tudor regime of Henry VII, and tomb of Sir Rhys ap Thomas.

FIGURE 14.6
Dryslwyn Castle remains, Carmarthenshire

Photo © Jeffrey L. Thomas

Earl of Cornwall surrounding the castle. Five years later Rhys ap Maredudd, who had escaped to Ireland, was betrayed, taken to York and executed in April of 1292. The ancient royal dynasty of Deheubarth, the lineage of Hywel Dda and Lord Rhys effectively died with him (39).

The castle Carreg Cennen (Fig. 14.7) on a Black Mountain escarpment is the most "splendidly situated" castle anywhere in Wales (4). It was largely a symbol of power rather than a military fortress. The castle was considered a Welsh stronghold. However, during the 12th century, at the time of Rhys ap Gruffudd, ruler of the kingdom of Deheubath, many of the territorial gains of the Normans were reversed. This castle and others near Lord Rhys' royal seat at Dinefwr and Dryslwyn faced down the Tywi Valley toward the Norman castle at Carmarthen. Carreg Cennen was rebuilt near the end of the 13th century, during the conquest of Wales by Edward I and then partially dismantled in 1461 by

Chapter 14—The Castles in Rhys History   115

FIGURE 14.7   Photo © Jeffrey L. Thomas
Carreg Cennen Castle, Carmarthenshire
ruins *(above)*; artist's rendering *(below)*

Yorkists during the Wars of the Roses.

The largest castle in Wales is the Caerffili (Fig. 14.8) near the town of the same name, just north of Cardiff (39). Covering about 30 acres, it has lake defenses, three drawbridges, and six pertcullises (iron gratings that can slide down over doorways) over double doors (4). Construction of the castle was begun in 1268 by Gilbert de Claire (1243–1295), a powerful English baron and of the Lord Marches of Glamorgan. DeClares' loyalty switched to the English King Henry III, and he drove out the local Welsh Lord Gruffudd ap Rhys, Lord of Senghennydd who owned the land

FIGURE 14.8
Caerffili Castle, Caerffili

Photo © Jeffrey L. Thomas

and at an earlier date began to build the castle. It took 58 years overall. Llewelyn ap Gruffudd, the son of Lord Rhys attacked and destroyed the new castle of deClares before it was finished. He was supported by a growing number of Welsh lords of upland Glamorgan. Gilbert deClare's son (also Gilbert), was killed in the battle of Bannockburn in 1314 and the castle passed to Eleanor, the granddaughter, and her husband Hugh le Despenser, a favorite of King Edward II (38). Llywelyn's men, including his two sons, besieged the castle but in the end surrendered. His sons and wife Lleucu, were imprisoned in the Tower of London at KingEdward II's command in 1316. Hugh le Despenser took Llywelyn into custody and in 1318 he was hung, drawn, and quartered in Cardiff. The native Welsh were not the only ones to feel disgust at this treatment. A number of English Marcher Lords also criticized le Despenser's barbarity (4).

The Carew Castle (Figs. 14.9, 14.14, pp. 2–3, and front cover) stands in a meadow by the River Carew in Pembrokeshire

FIGURE 14.9
Carew Castle, Pembrokeshire (principle residence of Sir Rhys ap Thomas)

(38). Built between 1280 and 1310 on the site of a Norman motte mound and bailey double walled structure, it incorporates "maisonettes" used by the chaplain and constable of the garrison. Although Sir Rhys ap Thomas's properties included castles at Narberth (Fig. 14.10), Newcastle Emyln (Fig. 14.11), and Weobley (p. *v*), his principal residence was Carew Castle where he added sumptuous new lodgings embellished with Tudor royal heraldry. In the late 16th century Sir John Perrot, an illegitimate son of Henry VIII added a magnificent new wing (35). The Rhys family had lost their inheritance, confiscated by King Henry VIII after the execution of Rhys ap Gruffudd in 1531. The Sir Rhys Jousting Tournament extravaganza, now called an Eisteddfod (treated in another chapter) was carried out at Carew Castle and park area in 1506.

In the northern province of Gwynedd, the castle Dolwyddelan (Fig. 14.12) became a part of Edward I's of England chain of defense fortifications. It was earlier occupied by Llywelyn ap

FIGURE 14.10
Narberth Castle remains, Pembrokeshire

Iorvwerth (the Great), Prince of Gwynedd, and a descendant of Owain Gwynedd and Gruffudd ap Cynan who were formidable leaders. As Llywelyn built more castles, his power increased. The unpopular King John followed his brother King Richard I and reigned 1199–1216. His English troops and rival Welsh Lords including Rhys Gryg of Deheubarth marched into Gwynedd and eventually forced Llywelyn to surrender (39). Rhys Gryg's name means Rhys the Hoarse.

Dinefwr Castle (Fig. 14.13), known as the stronghold of the

FIGURE 14.11
Newcastle Emlyn Castle remains, Carmarthenshire

FIGURE 14.12
Dolwyddelan Castle remains, Gwynedd

Photo © Jeffrey L. Thomas

House of Rhys, was the home of the families of Rhys ap Tewdwr, the Lord Rhys, and Rhys ap Thomas for most of the decades between the 11th and 16th centuries. Prior to that the castle witnessed the martial pomp of the royal Rhgodri and the graver dignity of the court of Howel the Good (51). From here Rhys ap Tewdwr sounded the shrill trumpet to call his forces to arms to meet the Normans.

> Gruffydd ap Rhys went forth from Dinefwr castle to slay the 3,000 Flemings and French on the banks of the Teivi in the early 12th century. The Lord Rhys called this seat his own when he confounded the Normans in their councils, scattered their forces, expelled their lords from half a dozen castles and compelled King Henry II to yield him the title of Lord of South Wales (51).

FIGURE 14.13
Dinefwr Castle, Carmarthenshire

Photo © Jeffrey L. Thomas

In *History of Wales* by John Davies (3), reference is made to the house of Rhys. In 1283 the land holdings of Rhys ap Maredudd were augmented so that they extended from the River Aeron to the River Tywi. He was disappointed by the English king's decision to take into his own hands the royal seat of Dinefwr and most of the territories owned by those members of the house of Deheubarth who had remained loyal to Llywelyn. Rhys's communities were soon drawn into the web of royal authority. Rhys Wyndod, lord of Dinefwr at the time, and Rhys Fychau, lord of northern Ceredigion were imprisoned. Maelgwn, the son of Rhys Fychau, died in the revolt of 1294 which was part of the discontent following King Edward I's conquest of Wales in 1277–1282.

The history relating to the Welsh castles is an interesting study in and of itself.

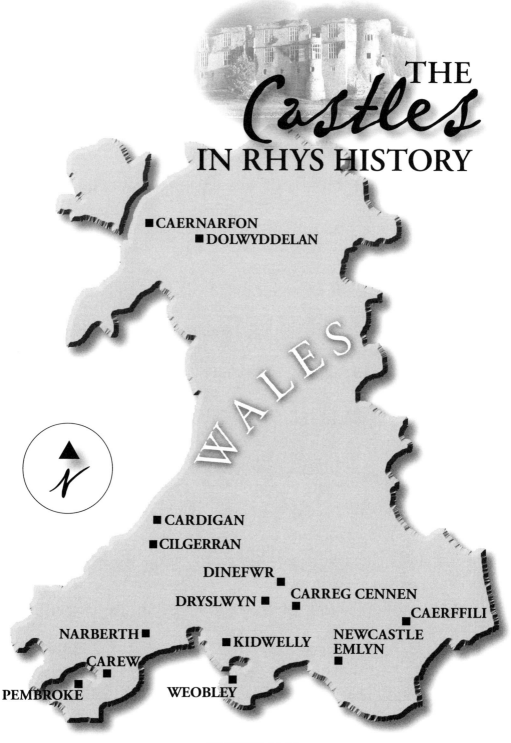

FIGURE 14.14
Relative locations of chapter 14 castles

15
SIR RHYS AP THOMAS

A RENOWNED figure in Welsh and English history, Sir Rhys ap Thomas (1449–1525), is considered to be the ancestor of many Rees families coming to America. His offspring may have numbered as many as twenty; all of which were well provided for upon his demise (35).

As a young man of genteel heritage, Prince Rhys became a popular leader by his stature and bravery, including a mastery of horsemanship and skill with the long bow. From his aristocratic background he exhibited an interest in cultural events. As noted elsewhere the Rhys name is prominent in Welsh history from the earliest times. It is also evident that Rhys and his ancestors had received an education offered by the clerics of their time.

Among the many historical accounts relating to Sir Rhys ap Thomas, the details leading to his support of the Earl of Richmond, who was to become Henry VII, is well recorded in *Annals and Antiquities of the Counties and County Families of Wales (51)*. Some excerpts from this lengthy and detailed account, leading to the final battle of the Wars of the Roses, are given in subsequent paragraphs.

While the Earl of Richmond was born in Pembroke Castle, and Anglesey was the cradle of the Royal House of Tudor, the castle of Brecon witnessed the concoction of the scheme, which placed Henry VII on the English throne. Carmarthen claims a chief hand in bringing the plan to pass, done through the efforts of the "illustrious" Rhys ap Thomas of Dinefawr Castle.

The family of Rhys ap Tewdwr of the house of Dinefawr in the late 11th century diminished; however, Sir Rhys ap Thomas represented the Dinefawr Castle in the 15th century with an influence similar to his princely ancestors. Richard III, the English king, considered his friendship with Rhys of utmost importance. He was the owner of enormous tracts of the Welsh countryside.

Sir Rhys was also a man who valued popularity and power. This remarkable man, says the author of the *Annals,* established an almost feudal government of his estates, but with the entire absence of force or fear. On his manors of Carew, Narberth, Emlyn, and others, he adopted a plan of rearing horses, which he distributed as gifts among his tenants, coupling with the gift a kind of military service. It is said in a biography of him written at the time of King James I, that his tenants numbered, in the author's words,

> . . . between eighteen and nineteen hundred, and all of them bound by

their leases to be readie with a horse when he called upon them.

Again, in the words of the biographer, he was, by his wide influence

> ... able to bring into the field a 4,000 or 5,000 horse military force upon a varie shorte summons, which popularitie of his, had happened in the time of a jealouse and umbragiouse prince, might easilie have wrought his confusion; but Edward IV (r. 1461–1483) being well assured of the loiall intentions of his hart, thought himself happie in the strength of so powerful a subject.

The biographer in these statements was writing of the time when Rhys ap Thomas was in his early thirties, with one son. At about age thirty-seven he was knighted by Henry VII. The biographer goes on,

> ... neither did the people suffer their desires here to rest, for as he gave them horses, soe they gave him certain patches of land with their estates, and at their verie doores (as if in some doting or roving humour they intended to erect some newe tenure to envassal themselves unto him); and this they did nott onlie for his countenance and protection, but to express likewise the interest he had in their hartes to love him, hands to fight for him, and in their fortunes to supplie all his occasions.

So eminent was Sir Rhys ap Thomas in the estimation of his countrymen that he was habitually called "Rhys fawr Cymry;" and the bard, Rhys Nanmor, did not aptly describe the extent of his possessions when he said,

> "Y brenin biar ynys (The island is divided in two pieces),
>
> Ond sy o ran I Syr Rhys (The larger the King's, the other, Sir Rhys")

Quoting from the *Annals (51)*,

> When foul weather broke on the tyrant, King Richard III, and rumors floated about that the Earl of Richmond was about to land at Milford Haven (coming from exile in Brittany) and claim the throne, the king lost no time in securing from Rhys ap Thomas a definite avowal of loyalty." Commissioners were sent to contact Rhys and "to take of him an oath of fidelitie and further, "requiring his onlie sonne, Gruffydd ap Rhys (Giffith Rice), as a gage for the true performances, etc.

A long letter was written to the king in the presence of the commissioners with a clear reluctance with regard to his "onlie sonne" who was only four or five at the time. But with his oath, He promised more than he afterwards performed. The letter is lengthy—over 800 words—and little known but very interesting. One statement reads,

> My conscience binds me to love and serve my King and country. My vowe can do no more.

It is dated Carmarthen Castle, 1484.

In addition to asserting Sir Rhys' loyalty, the letter states many thoughts including

> Whoever ill affected to the state shall dare to land in those parts of Wales where I have anie emploiments under your Majestie, must resolve with

> himself to make his entrance and
> irruption over my bellie.

The signature was Rice ap Thomas (English).

Over the ensuing months Sir Rhys felt the suspicion from

> ... a quarter so despicable as King
> Richard's nursed himself into posi-
> tive discontent, a process diligently
> assisted by the friends of the Earl of
> Richmond.

Some powerful clergy, the Bishop of St. David's, and the Abbot of Talley, gave advice—at first cautious, then open—in favor of Richmond, "the Lord's anointed," exclaimed the bishop.

> You have a King who is a cruel ty-
> rant, a bloodie butcher, a most unjust
> usurper, another Nero—always unsafe
> to do well.

Sir Rhys was not displeased at these words, saying,

> I pray what think you of the othe I
> have taken?

The bishop somewhat enlarged himself on the nature of a vowe:

> ... to be broken or kept, as it is good
> or bad in its foundation." "Holie
> David vowed rashlie to Abigail and
> yet David broke that vowe and God
> and all good men allowed thereof for
> well donn ...

But the vow declared that no invader should land without having to pass over his body. The bishop had his reply:

> I shall never hold it for any disparage-
> ment to your humilitie, to lay yourself
> prostrate on the ground for the true
> and indubitate loard of all (Earl of
> Richmond) to make an easie entrance
> over you!

The author of the *Annals* goes on about this moment in English history which may conclude the Wars of the Roses with Sir Rhys taking further counsel with the bishop, the abbot, friends such as Morgan of Cydweli, Armond Butler, Richard Griffith, and John Moran, "old and experienced soldiers." Their discordant was of little help, knowing that an immediate breach with the king may bring an end to his young life.

An "autographed" letter came from the Earl of Richmond in Brittany, praying for Rhys' cooperation, including letters of aid from several important quarters. Sir Rhys, now nearly ready to change his mind, took one more step of precaution. He consulted his friend and prophet "Robert of the Dale" and insisted on knowing whether Richmond's cause would or would not prevail. Was there hope of reward or was there nothing but death awaiting him? Upon being consulted, Robert of the Dale answered:

> Hie thee to the Dale, I'll to the vale
> to drink gude ale, and soe I pre have a
> care of us all.

This was interpreted to mean that Richmond would land at Dale, near Milford, and that the lives and fortunes of all the people were in Sir Rhys ap Thomas' hands.

Soon he became determined and was joined by a number of magnates, some from the north including the noble "Robert Salisburie." A hundred horses were brought out of his own stables. Sir Rhys mounted his charger, Grey-Fetler-Locks, "in a most martial manner" towards the Dale, a place not far from his castle of Carew (51).

He was in time to receive Richmond, just landing, and tendered him at once his service and the service of all his followers. Mindful of the bishop's lesson, he laid himself prostrate on the ground and suffered the earl to step over him, thus making good his promise to King Richard and keeping a good conscience (51).

The Earl of Richmond, Henry Tudor, came with French mercenaries and picking up support from Sir Rhys and knights of his native Welsh countryside, positioned himself at Bosworth Field in central England. The forces of William Stanley to the north and Lord Stanley to the south, supported the king and remained in position until the archery dual was slowed. The king's forces under the Earl of Northumberland also withheld action for a time. Some marshland separated the battle elements.

As the forces of the Earl of Richmond moved to attack, the king mounted, collected his bodyguard around him, and rode into the center of the enemy, intent on killing Henry Tudor or dying like a king. Instead of supporting the king, the Stanleys attacked the flanks of the Northumberland forces. The king was "unhorsed" in the marsh and killed. Lord Stanley took the circlet indicating Richard's rank, from the king's helmet and placed it on Henry Tudor's head (27) thus ending the Wars of the Roses on August 22, 1485. Although the last major battle, various Yorkists caused the early years of King Henry Tudor's reign to be in continued danger (27).

It is said in the *Annals (51)* that Sir Rhys ap Thomas performed a distinguished part in the battle and was bountifully rewarded when Henry mounted the throne. Another author claims Rhys shot the arrow with the long-bow that killed King Richard. King Henry VII appointed him to the prefecture and chief government of Wales, which included Constable and Lieutenant of Brecknock; Chamberlain of South Wales in the counties of Carmarthen and Cardigan; Seneschal of the lordship of Builth, Haverfordwest, and Rhos; and Knight Banneret, Knight of the Garter, Privy Councillor. "With these honours and offices heaped upon him, Sir Rhys was commanded to go for Wales" (51).

For many years Sir Rhys continued to perform the duties of these and other offices in South Wales. He died in 1525 at age 76. He was buried in the Church of the Grey Friars in Friars' Park, but after the dissolution of the Friary in 1538, the tomb (Fig. 15.1) was removed to St. Peter's Church. In 1866 the Lord Dynevor, a direct descendant, restored the tomb of Sir Rhys ap Thomas of Dynevor (53).

The author of the *Annals* states,

> His remains, together with those of his ladie, nowe reste under a statelie monument, which, to do justice to his greate fame and honourable deservings, should have been "AEre perennius," but, sorrie am I to saie, is made of a sorte of freestone, of so softe a graine that it alreadie beares evident proofes of unfaithfulnesse . . . to the sculptor's art.

A more recent restoration makes it prim and fresh, but has lost thereby—

The pitted cheek and wrinkled brow, wise sentences inscribed by time.

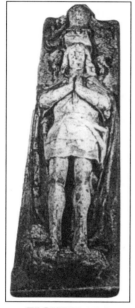

FIGURE 15.1 Tomb of Sir Rhys with his Lady Eva in Saint Peter's Church, Carmarthen

and therefore, some of its power to carry the mind to the long past. Sir Rhys ap Thomas' lady, who is also commemorated and here entombed, is said to be Eva, the daughter of Henry ap Gwilym of Court Henry (51).

Sir Rhys carefully provided for his family and 12 natural (illegitimate) offspring. Six years later, his prime heir fell victim to Henry VIII's suspicions and the family estates were forfeited to the crown. (See chapter 16, "The Great Betrayal.")

Charles Kightly, author of *Chieftains and Princes (35)* notes,

> Late medieval wielders of power were expected to display "largesse," translatable as "conspicuous consumption" or more prosaically, "showing off."

One of the foremost Welsh exponents of this practice was Sir Rhys ap Thomas, the leading magnate of early Tudor Southwest Wales. His position was greatly enhanced by joining Henry Tudor's march to victory at Bosworth Field in 1485. Kightly goes on to say,

> The proceeds of Henry VII's favour added considerable to Sir Rhys' sizable income from inherited estates. His properties included castles at Narberth, Newcastle Emlyn and Weobley prior to the gifts of Henry VII.

His office was at Carmarthen Castle and his principle residence was Carew Castle where he built sumptuous new lodgings embellished with Tudor royal heraldry. Sir Rhys's Carew was also an important focus of culture, attracting bards who compared it to King Arthur's Court. Some of its splendid furnishings still survive (Fig. 15.2) (35).

A unique Welsh cultural jamboree known as the *Eisteddfod*, or session, is a descendant of ancient bardic tournaments in which poets

FIGURE 15.2
Sir Rhys's "Garter Chair" bearing his Garter arms (by permission of the National Museum of Wales, Welsh Folk Museum).

and musicians competed for a seat of honor in the households of noblemen. This was a highly prized position since poets depended on patronage for their livelihood (4).

The first genuinely regional tournament was held in 1176 at Rhys ap Gruffydd's castle in Cardigan. A most notable event of this kind was also held by Sir Rays ap Thomas at his Carew Castle in 1506 to celebrate his election as Knight of the Garter.

In the "Memoir" of Sir Rays printed in the *Cambrian Register* (1796), is a long description of the celebrations. From it we learn that Sir Rays ap Thomas made announcement of a "solemn and joust tournament," the fame of which being blown abroad.

> Maine worthy and valerouse gentlemen of his blood, some to do him honor and some to make triall of their abilities in feats of armes, came unto him from all partes of Wales.
>
> They rode in on their caparisoned chargers, the Herberts, Perrotts, Wogans, Butlers, Gruffydds, Morgans, Dunns, Vaughans (of Tretwr), Jenkin Mansel "the valiant" (of Oxwich); from North Wales, Griffith, son of Sir John Griffith, Lord of Llansadwrn, and young Wynn of Gwydir, "two hopeful gentlemen of good towardsinesse, and with them the lustie Robert Salisburie, a man noted for his great strength of bodie, a fast friend and companion of Sir Rhys in many of his warlike adventures" (51).

These men of "prime ranke" were all lodged within the castle. For some 500 more, "most of them of good ranke and qualitie," tents and pavilions were pitched in the castle park.

This festival and "time of jollitie" continued for five days.

On St. Georges Eve it began, when Sir Rhys took a view of all the company, choosing out 500 of the tallest and ablest of them, dividing them into five troops and placing each troop under the direction of a captain. The second day was occupied in exercising the troops in the field "in all points as if they were suddenly to go on some notable service." The third day the drummers beat up, the trumpets sounded, the whole host came forth as in battle array "well armed at all points." They marched to the bishop's palace at Lamphey, a mile or thereabouts distance from Carew,

> ... bidd goode morrowe to the bishoppe in the language of souldiers with arquebusses, musketts and callivers, the bishop, having with him the abbot of Talley and the prior of Carmarthen, "all with rich capes."
>
> After some mock parley the business being so ordered aforehand, gave entrance to Sir Rhys. The bishop ascended to the high altar, read devine service, and new hymns were sung "for the reste of St. George's soule and his safe deliverance out of purgatorie" (51).
>
> On the return of the cavalcade to Carew a grand solemnity of dining took place, bishop and abbot being of the company. The "sewer" (medieval household officer of high rank in charge of seating, serving, and tasting) being the host's son, Sir Griffith ap Rhys, who had binn bredd up at coorte, and had some advantage of the others in point of curialitie and courtliness;" Sir William Herbert of Coldbrook as the carver, and "young

Griffith of Penrhyn the pocillator or cupbearer" (51).

The music went on: "hautboies (oboes) and other wind instruments were not silent." The bishop said grace and the dinner began. The health of king, queen, and prince are "often drank." Bards and pyrdydds accompanied by the harp sang many a song. After the entertainment "they walke abroad and take the fresh aire of the parke" and lastly, in the chapel, "heare solemne service" (51).

The next day, the real day of joust and tournament, Sir William Herbert's challenge to all comers, four to four, "for the honour of ladies" was presently accepted by Sir Griffith Rhys. Sir Rhys "on a goodlie steed, in fine gilt armour, two pages on horseback before him with a herauld" was judge of the jousts.

The trumpets sounded and the knights presented themselves for the conflict, each with his device and motto displayed.

> The two first combattants putt their launces into their restes, and soe rann each theire six courses. In like sorte followed the reste" to the end of the brilliant tournament. "Sound knockes you may be sure were received and returned on both sides, butt no harme at all done (51).

At supper, Sir Griffith ap Rhys, age 26, in the presence of his father, made challenge to Sir William Herbert, four to four, at the ring next morning. It was for a supper which the losers should pay for at Carmarthen for their farewell at parting. The challenge was accepted and the loser, by his father's judgment was Sir Griffith ap Rhys, a thing "agreed upon beforehand," as the careful narrator tells us, "that soe he might show his friendes the towne of Carmarthen before they went away."

Carmarthen must have been a fine place in those days! After dinner, Sir Rhys ap Thomas gave his guests a hunt in the park, where "they killed divers buckes" destined to be consumed at the Carmarthen supper. The supper ended this memorable and unique tournament—a strange medley of healthful and knightly pastime, religious observance, and chivalric gallantry. One thing the conscientious chronicler declares,

> It is note-worthie that for the space of five days, among a thousand people, there was not one quarrell, crosse worde or unkind look that happened" (51).

Early in the morning before they parted, we must also observe "the bishoppe bestowed a sermon upon them tending to all loyall admonitions, obedience to superiors, love and charitie one towards another." His text was out of Ecclesiastes 10:20—

> Curse not the king, no, not in thy thoughts, and curse not the rich in thy bedd-chamber.

Sir Rhys ap Thomas, Kt (Knight) of Dinefwr was, at the turn of the century, proprietor of the lordship of Dinefwr, Carew, Llansadwrn, Cilsane, Emlyn, Cilcenin, Aberayron, Llanrhystyd, Narberth, Llangybi, and two or three others. Little has been recorded about his family other than that they were well provided for upon his death in 1525 at age 76. A son, three daughters, and the grandson—chosen as his heir—have been mentioned in the literature. The grandson, of course, is the subject of the next chapter, "The Great Betrayal."

16
THE GREAT BETRAYAL

IN THE annals of world history, as noted elsewhere, there has been great turmoil every 500 years. The Reformation, the greatest event in church history, began in 1517 and played itself out in the next century-and-a-half. England was in the throes of establishing herself as a power to contend with in the awakening world. King Henry VIII authorized the first substantial navy, England's differences with France continued, and the King's disagreements with the Pope of the Church of Rome (as well as his matrimonial problems) all added to the turmoil of the times as noted in Derek Wilson's *In the Lion's Court (18)*. Also as noted elsewhere, the Rhys ancestral line has been most prominent in Welsh history.

This continued to be true with Sir Rhys ap Thomas (1449–1525) who lived in these times and was greatly respected by his peers as a leader. He died in 1525, having carefully provided for his family, with twelve natural offspring (35). Due to his holdings in land and offices, Sir Rhys was considered a rival of Henry VIII. The King knew that Sir Rhys had been credited with putting his father on the throne by defeating the tyrant, Richard III. At Sir Rhys's death, the Rhys family inherited the estates, however most of the offices were granted to Walter Devereaux, the steward of the household of the king's daughter, Mary. In 1529 a quarrel arose between Devereaux's men and those of Rhys ap Gruffudd, the grandson of Sir Rhys, who now was head of the House of Dinefwr, long associated with the Rhys family.

King Henry VIII (reigning 1509–1547) had seen fit to sweep away potential claimants to the throne with a ferocity that would make Richard III appear tenderhearted. One of them was the Duke of Buckingham, executed in 1521. There then remained two men of substantial power in Wales: Sir Rhys ap Thomas and Charles Somerset. Charles Somerset was appointed to the earldom of Worcester in 1514, which changed his influence and scope of activity.

After the death of Sir Rhys, the king accused the grandson, Rhys ap Gruffudd, of plotting with the King of Scots to make himself ruler of Wales. Some of the evidence against him was that he had sought to stress his links with the ancient Welsh kings by adopting the name "Fitzurien." Rhys ap Gruffudd was executed in December 1531 (51), and his family estates were forfeited to the crown.

Author Gareth Elwyn Jones looks at the event from another perspective (12).

> When Sir Rhys died, the king

denied his heir, Rhys ap Gruffudd, the grandfather's office of "chamberlain of South Wales" saying he lacked experience. The king and his advisors appointed Lord Ferrers of Chartley, a major Herefordshire landowner, to succeed to the chambership and other lesser offices. The influence of Rhys ap Gruffudd's ambitious wife, together with Ferrer's arrogant attitude, produced an explosive situation. In June 1529 at a time of national difficulty with Henry VIII involved in the divorce problem, both Rhys ap Gruffudd and Ferrers were called to London to face charges. After a period in the Tower, Rhys was executed. His was not the only Tudor execution to take place on the flimsiest of evidence. It seems likely that his real crime was to be too closely associated with Cardinal Wolsey who was opposed to the annulment of Henry VIII's marriage with Catherine of Aragon.

In his *Studies in Welsh History,* J. F. Rees (20) discusses Tudor policy in Wales relating many details leading up to the assimilation of the country under the crown in 1536. Author Rees, as a Principal of the University College of South Wales, reviews events leading up to the battle of Bosworth Field on August 22, 1485, the role of Sir Rhys ap Thomas, and the misfortune of Rhys ap Gruffydd after his grandfather's death.

Quoting from the Rees work,

> Sir Rhys ap Gruffydd, a young man who had been educated at the English Court, was married to Lady Katherine Howard, daughter of the second duke of Norfolk and sister of the Victor of

Flodden Field. Either on account of his youth or because it seemed a suitable opportunity to break with the past, the public offices enjoyed by his grandfather were not conferred upon him.

Walter Devereaux and Lord Ferrers of Chartley, members of the Council of the Marches, were appointed Chief Justice and Chamberlain of South Wales. Trouble soon arose! In March 1529 Sir Rhys ap Gruffydd complained to Cardinal Wolsey of the high-handed conduct of some of Devereaux's officials towards his tenancy. When Devereaux arrived at Carmarthen early in June to hold the Sessions, a quarrel broke out between him and Sir Rhys about the quarters to be occupied by their respected retinues. Bickering seems to have continued for a week or more and culminated on the 15th of the month in a scene created by Sir Rhys, who entered the court with some armed attendants and demanded the release of one of his servants. Sir Rhys was himself taken into custody and later in the year the case against him was heard in London. What exactly happened subsequently will probably always remain obscure. It is certain that Sir Rhys was set at liberty and probably remained in London.

Continuing,

He was arrested and committed to the Tower in October 1530, but released the following June owing to the state of his health. At the end of September he was again sent to the Tower and charged with high treason. It was alleged that he was involved in a conspiracy to effect an uprising in Wales in conjunction with a Scottish invasion of England. But, apart from the evidence of an informer that he had given credence to a prophecy that King James of Scotland, 'with the Red Hand and the Ravens should conquer all England', there appears to have been no basis for the accusation.

Henry VIII had entered upon a critical period of his reign and charges of conspiracy, however flimsy their foundations, hardly needed proof. Sir Rhys, smarting under the sense of grievance, was probably guilty of no worse offense than uttering some wild words at an unguarded moment. He was executed on Tower Hill on 4 December 1531." The author in a note, indicates he believes the 'Red Hand' to be help from Ireland and the 'Ravens' refer to the coat of arms of Sir Rhys.

In the summer of 2002, the writer and wife, Barbara, visited England and Wales. Upon exiting the Tower of London, I asked the guard, a Yeoman Warder in "Beefeater" costume, if he was aware of the execution of a person named Rees or "R-H-Y-S" (spelling it out). His response was "Yes, and he was at least in the top 10." He also informed me that there was a list in a brochure available in the Beauchamps Tower, also called "Bloody Tower." I was not able to find a copy in a hurried return to the location's main desk.

Although the Rhys surname remains prevalent in Wales, the family of Sir Rhys ap Thomas disappeared from the ranks of gentry, or huge landowners. The name did emerge in Ireland, Holland, and Scotland, as well as England. Thomas Nicholas (51) in commenting on the foremost names in Carmarthenshire many ages ago, notes

> What inhabitant...who lived in the time when the ironclad warriors of Rufus (the Normans) passed through these parts, would believe that the race of Rhys ap Tewdwr would ever cease? However, there has been no known male descendant of that illustrious house of Dinefwr in existence for 400 years.

Rhys was widely held to be innocent, but the fact remained that the premier lauded family of southwest Wales had been toppled.

Cymru—"Land of Fellow Countrymen"

The identifying icon for the following section, *Part V—A Rhys Family in America,* is the Leek plant, another national symbol of Wales.

PART V
A Rhys Family in America

17
A DUTCH CONNECTION

 IN MANY respects, the Welsh of the sixteenth century were cut off from the rest of the world. They were largely illiterate and those who were literate were fluent only in Welsh. Exceptions were the families of landowners and other gentry who were often educated by the church. As noted earlier, Sir Rhys ap Gruffydd was educated in the English Courts. Years later an Anglicized Welshman, William Williams, a member of Parliament, cried, "If the Welsh had the same educational advantages as the Scots who did all their schooling in English, they would in no respect differ from the English."

This, in itself, would be good reason for any adventurous

young men to leave their homeland. In the case of the sons and grandsons of our most likely ancestor, Sir Rhys ap Thomas, it must have seemed to them that, although they may have had some material wealth, they could no longer expect any measure of respect from the domineering English Crown. They also probably understood that any success they might attain would be suspect in the mind of the Monarch.

Family historians have traced their Rees ancestry from Ireland, Scotland, England, and Wales to the United States. Many with the Rees name still live in each of these countries.

Dedicated historians have traced our Rees line to the province of Lippe in what is now Germany. The founder of the principality was Bernard I (1113–1144) Lord of Lippe. Lippe became a Republic in common with the rest of Germany in November 1918 following World War I. The Lippe River flows from the west slope of the Teutoburg Forest west to the right bank of the Rhine near Wesel. It is navigable more than 100 miles to just past the city of Lippestatt, an early trading center reached by the Dutch trading companies.

Looking at the times between 1535 and 1650 in the watery area between Wales and the German principalities, great changes were taking place. The age of the Viking raids had long since passed. Portugal's sea power was in decline, and the English were just beginning to prepare for colonial adventure. Some of the most enterprising people in the world in the 16th century were the Dutch. Their school of navigation and seamanship was the waters between the Baltic Sea and the Bay of Biscay.

The Netherlands in the late 16th century included the extensive lowlands of present day Holland, Belgium, Luxembourg, and into Germany and northern France as part of the Habsburg Empire of Charles V. It came under the political domination of

Spain in 1555 when Charles bequeathed it to his son, Philip, along with the Spanish Crown (11).

Prior to this the people had been left very much to themselves. They were sturdy, self-reliant people, hardened by centuries of "stemming the tide," or the sea, and reclaiming the land. The Rhine, Scheldt, Meuse, and dozens of other waterways crisscrossed the country carrying commerce to inland Europe. As many as 500 ships a day sailed out of Antwerp (11).

Netherlands became a clearinghouse of ideas. Its lower schools were unsurpassed. Its illustrious scholars and intellectuals, such as Erasmus, were renowned throughout Europe. Scholars and merchants brought new religious ideas such as Lutheranism, Anabaptism, and Calvinism. Calvinism soon appealed to the rich, whose frugality, hard work, and self-reliance had brought them success. The aristocracy, in time, also accepted Calvinism. Its doctrine of the elect gave moral support to all people under persecution (11).

After a truce with Spain in 1609, the Dutch trading empire covered most of the world. Few spectacles in modern history are more remarkable than the explosive expansion of Holland and Zeeland, two waterlogged provinces that form the heart of the Republic of the Netherlands.

A very great tragedy of this time was the Thirty Years' War (1618–1648), involving the Holy Roman Empire and the Protestant nations to the north. Destruction, desolation, and poverty in both cities and rural areas caused the population to shrink from 18 million to about five million. A large-scale emigration from Germany to America began following the war and continued for the next 200 years. The Netherlands was not heavily involved except when the truce with Spain expired in 1621. Some hostilities resumed. By 1648 Spain was exhausted. The Treaty of

Munster, as a part of the Treaty of Westphalia, ending the Thirty Years' War, also brought an end to the conflict with Spain which had been going on since 1548 and sometimes was known as the Eighty Years' War (11). Antwerp, then a city in Netherlands, was the financial capital of the world.

In the first half of the 17th century, regardless of the battles with Spain in the southern provinces, the Dutch continued to expand their commerce and their colonial empire. In addition

FIGURE 17.1
A Dutch sailing ship of the 17th century as used in their world trade empire and similar to that on which Andries Rees served as ensign with the Dutch West Indies Company. (Photo taken from a large wall painting on the *M/S Oosterdam* of the Holland America Line.)

to their possessions in the East and West Indies, they held New Amsterdam (later renamed New York) on the North American continent. By 1650 the Dutch fleet (example, Fig. 17.1) was twice the size of the English and French fleets combined, and Amsterdam was the richest city in Europe (11).

The Dutch position inevitably led to a rivalry with England. England's Navigation Act of 1651 was aimed to curtail Dutch trade. Neither side was able to score a decisive victory in the sea war of 1652–1654. In the Treaty of Biceda the Dutch ceded New Amsterdam to the British for some British holdings in the Caribbean. Thus the procreator of the first Rees family in America is revealed as Andries Rees of Lippestadt (now Germany), a Dutch trading post of the 17th century.

An interesting note appears in the DAR Library record of *German Immigrants in New York, 1630–1674*. It says in part,

> Andries Rees, from Lippstadt, was one of the signers of the petition of the Lutherans of (New) Amsterdam, 1657, requesting that Rev. Goetwater be permitted to remain as Lutheran minister in the city. His wife was Ciletje Jans. Johannes, their second son, was baptized in New Amsterdam on April 25, 1656.

Andries, as noted elsewhere, was a soldier with the Dutch West Indies Company and in 1657 was promoted to the "rank of cadet."

Again, quoting the DAR record,

> When the government desired to billet-off soldiers in 1665, Andries, being approached, said he could take no soldiers because he is afraid of being robbed.

> He was engaged in tapping in 1660 and afterwards was several times arrested for tapping and playing at nine pins on holidays.
>
> When arrested in 1663, he admitted that he had "tapped on Sunday," but "after the preaching," which he was entitled to. Moreover, he did "no business during the week." He was liberated. In 1674 he had property on William Street, then known as Smith Street. (Tapping has a large number of meanings in the dictionary, starting with shoe repair.)

Andries, later ranked as an ensign with the trading company, was married to Celitje Jans, as noted, of Dutch ancestry. Their first son, Willem, married Catrina Janse also of Dutch ancestry. They had five sons. A daughter-in-law of record was Ariaantje Scherp, also of Dutch ancestry. The following generation's daughter-in-law was Rebecca Prys, Prys being a Welsh name. Coming into more modern times Johannes married Mareitje (Mary) Spoor, the fourth child of Jacob Spoor and Fytjen Hollenbeck. Marie A. Underwood compiled additional information on this family in 1901 entitled, *The Spoor Family in America*, also of Dutch ancestry.

Jacob Rees, one of the thirteen children of Johannes and Mareitje was born in Egremont, Massachusetts. Jacob married Anna Gillett on January 2, 1791 in West Stockbridge. Anna Gillett brought great talent and respect to the Rees family. The Gillett family is the basis for the discussion in the next chapter, *A French Connection*.

18

A FRENCH CONNECTION

OVER the centuries people with many surnames have contributed their qualities to the Rees family. We have seen the industrious Protestant influence of the Dutch. Another important contributing surname is Gillet, also spelled in various ways as Gylet, Galet, Gilett, Gillette, and others.

Much of the Huguenot immigration to America, according to Rev. William Gilet, son of Rev. Jacques Gilet, de Bergerac, the ancestor of the Gillett family in America, is known to have come from the town of Bergerac, Guyenne, France. In consequence of his continuing to preach the gospel, he was banished, his property confiscated and his life put in imminent danger.

The Gillet family in America is descended from two brothers, Jonathan and Nathan of Devonshire, England, sons of Huguenot parents who fled from their home near Burge, France to Scotland after 1572.

A sermon by a monk in 1560 declared that the Lutheran Protestants of France ought to be called Huguenots in that they assembled at the gate of King Hugo and only went out at night as he did. It is noteworthy that as early as 1512 Jacobus Faber enunciated the cardinal doctrine of reform, "justification by faith," and in 1525 his translation of the New Testament into French was completed. Also, in 1525 the first martyrs were burned at the stake; however, no persecution would ever stop the reform movement (59).

On January 29, 1535 an edict was published ordering the extermination of the heretics which resulted in a general emigration. Three years later the first French Protestant church, composed of 1,500 refugees, was founded in Strabourg. The most famous of these exiles was John Calvin, the future leader of the movement. Within a year, John Calvin fled to Basle where he wrote the famous *Institutio Christianae Religionio* and pleaded by letter to Francis I to respect the cause of the reformers. Completing the first edition, published in 1526, Calvin set out to show that the martyrs he had seen burned, some of them his friends, died for their belief in justification by faith—the doctrine of the Reformation. First published in Latin, the little book was revised and published in other languages and finally became a large manual of Reformation teaching. So, Calvin defended the cause of his dying friends and justified their innocence to the nations of Europe (55). More recently his works have been summarized in *Instructions in Christianity* by J. P. Wiles.

By 1550 there was a remarkable increase in the reform movement and within two years there were 2,150 churches. The struggle now entered the arena of national politics and serious strife continued until the Edict of Nantes on April 13, 1598.

After the Peace of St. Germain, on August 8, 1570, peace seemed to be assured. However, on the night of August 24, 1572 there occurred the Massacre of St. Bartholomew's Day in which Coligny, the leader of the Protestant army, and all the leading Huguenots were slain (58).

The Huguenots were a select class of people, perhaps the most intelligent and enterprising Frenchmen in the 16th and 17th centuries. Few others came to America so gifted and prepotent as the French Huguenots. They had the same affinity for ideals and the tenacity of character as the founders of New England. With their French blood however, they brought sensibility, a creative fervor and an artistic endowment of their own (59).

The Rev. Jacques de Gylet is the earliest known ancestor of this branch of the Gillet family in America. He was born in 1549 in Bergerac, Guyenne, France. He married Jeanne Mestre, born in 1552. It is reported they were married in the French Church in Crispin, England. The record shows their son William Gylett was born in 1574, also in Bergerac, Guyenne, France, before they escaped to Scotland.

William Gylett, as a reverend, was "instituted" to the benefice of Rector of Chaffcombe, County Somerset, England on February 4, 1609. He died there early in 1641. He married in 1601 (spouse unknown) and fathered eight children, including Nathan and Jonathan who came to America in 1630. The children used the surname Gillet. His will fails to mention his eldest daughter or his wife, as proved April 16, 1641 in Somerset England (59).

Jonathan, and Nathan Gillet, early settlers in Windsor, Connecticut, were the progenitors of the Gillet families in America. On March 20, 1630 in company with 140 Puritans from the counties of Devonshire, Dorsetshire, and Sommersetshire, England, the brothers sailed with Rev. John Warham and Rev. John Mavericks as pastors, on the ship *John and Mary*. They arrived off Nantasket, Massachusetts on May 30, 1630, first settling in Dorchester, Massachusetts. Nathan and Jonathan moved to Windsor, Connecticut in 1636 where they remained for many decades (61).

Jonathan Gillet, Sr. was born in 1604 in England. He returned to England in 1634 to marry Miss Dolbere (Dolbiar) on March 29, 1634. She was born June 7, 1607 in England. They were married in Colyton, Devonshire, England. They remained in England a year before sailing on the ship *Recovery of London* from Weymouth, England in March 1635. How he met a girl from Colyton is not known, however, a *John and Mary* passenger named George Hull of Crewkerne, had two brothers who were ministers at Colyton. Jonathan and Mary became the parents of ten children. Jonathan was chosen a Windsor constable in 1665. He died at about age 77. Indians had killed two sons, Joseph at age 34 in 1675 at Bloody Brook, and Samuel in 1676 at age 34 at Turners Falls (61).

According to *Genealogies and Biographies—The Gillett Family (63)*, Thomas Gillet, the son of Jonathan Jr., or Thomas Gillet, the son of John Gillet, is the true progenitor of the Gillet to Rees line. John Gillet was the younger brother of Jonathan Jr., born October 6, 1644. He married Mary Barber July 8, 1669 and they had seven children: John, Thomas, Samuel, Nathaniel, Benjamin, Mary and Mercy. They were all listed with the surname spelled "Gillett." John was born October 5, 1644 in Dorchester, Massachusetts and died February 27, 1697.

Thomas, the son of John and Mary Barber Gillett, married Hannah Clark on February 26, 1704. Their children were Abel, Joel, and Jonah.

Sergeant Jonah Gillett, born October 18, 1708 in Windor, Connecticut, married Elizabeth Granger ("Hoskins" on a Gillett chart) on August 14, 1728. They were the parents of 12 children: Jonah, Jr., Elizabeth, Joel, Margery, Rachel, Tryphena, Simeon, Mercy, Thomas, Thomas, Lucy, and Thomas, a third son by that name due to the early death of the first two. Lucy was a twin to the second Thomas (63).

Simeon, the seventh child, third son of Sergeant Jonah Gillett, was born in Wintonbury, Connecticut on October 16, 1743. He married Rebecca Andrews on May 20, 1762 and resided in Canaan, Columbia County, New York as of 1790 (date of first census). There were seven children born to Simeon and Rebecca Andrews Gillet: Jeremiah, Polly, Simeon Jr., James, Anna, Dorcas, and Sarah. Anna, the second daughter was born July 14, 1773 in Canaan, Columbia County, New York. She became the key person bringing the Gillett family heritage to the Rees family when she married Jacob Rees on January 11, 1791 in West Stockbridge, Massachusetts. Anna's great pioneer strength and talent were evident throughout her long life (59).

19
PIONEERS
NEW AMSTERDAM WESTWARD

THE DUTCH explorer, Peter Minuit, landed on present-day Manhattan Island in 1626, and named it New Amsterdam. Less than three decades later Andries Rees, a soldier with the Dutch West Indies Company arrived in New Amsterdam with his wife and young son, Willem. They resided on Smits Street (now Williams Street) in what is now the Wall Street area. Andries was promoted to the rank of Cadet in June 1657 and continued with the West Indies Company. Prior to the British gaining control of New Amsterdam in 1674, Andries Rees took an oath of allegiance to the King of England in 1664.

Andries Rees, his wife Celitje Jans and son, Willem, were

the first of this Rees family, or possibly any Rees family in the New World. Celitje Jans was of Dutch ancestry. (A number of other Rees immigrants came to Philadelphia and the Carolinas in the 18th century.) A second son, Johannes, was born in New Amsterdam and baptized April 26, 1656.

Lippstadt on the Lippe River, running west to the Rhine from what is now Germany, was given as the birthplace of Andries Rees. The Thirty Years War (1618–1648) had devastated large areas of the princedoms, duchies or provinces which became a united Germany after the Treaty of Frankfort in 1871.

Willem Andries Rees, born about 1651 in Lippstadt (now Germany) in a section of northwest Europe known as the "Lowlands" before Netherlands, Belgium, Luxembourg, Germany, or even Denmark, became well-defined nations. The cultural and geographic homogeneity and language of Holland and northern German provinces were close enough to be mutually understandable. There were no natural boundaries.

Following the death of his father sometime after 1674 in New Amsterdam, and possibly in the service of the West Indies Company, Willem, his mother, and brother migrated up the Hudson River Valley to the town of Claverac. There he married Catrina Janse in about 1670. They had at least eight children. The record shows that Willem became a naturalized citizen of the colony of New York on January 17, 1716. In 1720 he became known as "Willem of Claverac." After the death of Catrina, in 1721, he married Maria Goeway.

Andries Rees, probably the eldest of Willem's five sons, was born about 1677 in Fort Orange, New York, along the Hudson River. Like his father, Andries became known as "Andries Rees of Claverac" and also as a "Freeholder of Albany County." Many in the family became Livingston Manor tenants and very early settlers of the "Taghconic" area before it became part of the towns of Mt. Washington and Sheffield in the southwest corner of Massachusetts. After the "Livingston Uprising," most migrated to the Egremont, Massachusetts area.

On January 1, 1697 (date uncertain), Andries married Ariaantje Scherp. She was born about 1667 in Kinderhook, Columbia County, New York of Dutch ancestry.

In the 17th century as the Rees families moved up the Hudson River Valley, they came in contact with more English speaking people. Although the family surname "Rees" prevailed in most cases, there were some who chose to spell their name in English as it sounded when spoken in Dutch or German. This is the explanation of why a few sons chose the surname "Race." To prevent confusion, some genealogists prefer to carry the "Race" name in parenthesis or as "Rees/Race" (44).

Andries and Ariaantje Rees had at least two sons, Willem and Andries. Willem was killed April 15, 1755 while resisting an attempt by Livingston men to evict him from his home. There were many misunderstandings in regard to property purchased from the Indians. Andries reportedly was born January 7, 1699 in Albany County, New York (44).

Andries Janse Rees married Rebecca Prys on October 2, 1732 in the Dutch Reformed Church in Catskill, just west of the Hudson River in New York. Rebecca was born in 1713. Andries was one of a group who purchased a large tract of land from the Stockbridge Indians in a deed dated November 25, 1756, and like his father, was involved in the "Livingston Uprising." Andries and Rebecca had at least two sons, Johannes (John) and Nicholas. Nicholas chose to take the surname "Race." Johannes was born March 9, 1735 in Tackanic, New York. The Andries Rees family moved to Egremont, Massachusetts where both died; Andries on December 14, 1768 and Rebecca on November 5, 1801 at age 88.

Johannes "John" Rees was baptized in the Linlithgo Reformed Church of Livingston. John became a farmer and reportedly served as a "Minuteman" in local skirmishes in the Revolutionary War. Many that served in this manner were not recorded as soldiers and returned to their homes until called again. John Rees is listed in the *DAR Patriot Index* as a Private, New York, in the Revolutionary War.

John Rees married Mary (Mareitje) Spoor (born October 30, 1743) on June 30, 1761 in Egremont, Massachusetts. Mary was the forth child of Jacob Spoor and Fytie Hollenbeck, of Dutch ancestry. John and Mary had 13 children, three being born after moving to West Stockbridge. They, with John's brother, Nicholas Race, came to the southern end of Maple Hill and settled on lots two and three south of the Benjamin Lewis property. The record shows that

> In 1768 David Naunauneekanuck deeded lots two and three to Johnannis and Nicholas Race/Rees of Egremont" They paid Cornelius VanSchaack of Kinderhook, New York one hundred pounds toward discharging the Indians' "just debts."

Mary Spoor Rees died December 3, 1793, at age 50. John Rees was listed in the first census of the United States, Berkshire County, Massachusetts, 1790 as a family with three male persons over age 16, three male persons under age 16, and five female family members.

In a book of family history, collected by Miles Rees Moffatt, appears this statement,

While residing near the railroad, Grandpa (Isaac Miles Rees, 1798–1887, grandson of the early settler John Rees of Maple Hill in 1768) ran an old fulling mill at the lower dam on the west bank of the Williams River opposite the old stone mill standing then. Marble was being quarried on a large scale in all parts of town by 1790. The fulling mill is used to treat cloth by a shrinking process to make it "full" or dense. Isaac Rees built the mills on the west side of the river in the mid 1800's for carding, dressing cloth and for grinding plaster (9).

In the bicentennial publication, *West Stockbridge, Massachusetts*, where many religious denominations are listed along with some of their local history, it is noted that John Rees and two other prominent residents are listed as Episcopalians. Religious life was important in the early days of West Stockbridge. The town was incorporated in 1774, some 50 years after western Massachusetts was opened to settlers. They built the first meeting house in January 1776. Edna Bailey Garnetts, with many names and pictures, interestingly narrated the history of this small town (9).

Jacob Rees, son of John Rees and Mary Spoor, was born March 24, 1768, the same year they moved to West Stockbridge. On January 2, 1791 Jacob married Anna Gillett, the daughter of Simeon Gillett and Rebecca Andrews. They started their life together in West Stockbridge where their first two children, Jacob Singer and Rebecca, were born.

Anna's father, Simeon Gillett, was chosen to be a military officer by the special town meeting on November 10, 1774 concurring with an act of the Provincial Congress to organize a militia. Also chosen were three other officers, four sergeants, two drummers, and four corporals. The officers were a Captain, a Lieutenant, an Ensign, and Simeon Gillett as Clerk. The town was only two months old when the First Continental Congress met in Philadelphia on September 5, 1774. Anna's ancestors, the Gillett family, are reviewed in the previous chapter, *A French Connection*.

In the spring of 1794 Jacob Rees left his wife and two children to seek property in central New York State where land was still available. One historical note claims he went on horseback whereas another said he walked and often had to chop his way through the wilderness. He selected a homesite (see Fig. 19.1) near the Chenango River, cleared an acre of land and built a log cabin.

FIGURE 19.1
Stone Lodge Farm (1988), Route 12, a mile north of Sherburne, built about 1814 by the pioneers Jacob and Anna Gillet Rees. The house stands close to the site of the Rees early log cabin.

Jacob then returned to West Stockbridge, a trip of over one hundred fifty miles.

> In 1795 Jacob returned to the cabin with his wife Anna and their two small children. The young family traveled from Stockbridge by ox-cart.

Quoting from a magazine article on local old stone homes,

> Eight more Rees children were born after the family settled near Sherburne. Anna, a Stockbridge school teacher before her marriage, raised her large family and also continued her career. She became the 'first lady school teacher' in Otsego County. Her active life agreed with this remarkable woman. She lived to the age of 102.

She was often honored at the Rees–Gillett reunions held each year in the latter part of the nineteenth century, as noted in the next chapter.

The eight additional children of Jacob and Anna Rees, born after Jacob and Rebecca, were John Melancthon, Martha L., Simeon Gillett, Otto Andrew, Anna, Mary, Sarah C., and Caroline D. Jacob died April 8, 1830 at age 62 after 39 years of marriage. In her later years Anna married Nathaniel Bacon (44). Otto stayed on the homestead with his mother and married Mary Ann Race. They raised a family of six children.

The two older brothers, Jacob Singer and John Melancthon, married the Mills sisters, Anna and Angeline, respectively, in Sherburne, New York in 1820. Historical research on the Gillett family by Grace M. Steeves indicates John Melancthon Rees, at age 17, served in the War of 1812 from New York State and drew a pension from the U.S. government.

Sometime after the death of their father, Jacob and John, with their families, joined a covered wagon train of eight families south of Utica, that traversed the "Great Genesee Road" west toward Buffalo and along the coast of Lake Erie to Cleveland and beyond. Leaving the coast of Lake Erie and heading west, they found the population to be increasingly sparse. Upon reaching the St. Joseph River Valley, they encountered a few more people, including Indians, and decided to claim some land. The trip took about three weeks. John and Angeline brought their eight children, between the ages of 12 and one year. They traveled in the spring or early summer of 1834 and settled in the area that is now Milton Township, just east of Niles, Michigan.

Brother Jacob Singer and his wife, Anna Mills Rees, settled in nearby Ontwa Township. They traveled with their three children—all girls—ages 12 and older. A son, Jacob R., was born in Michigan and by 1860 had become the owner of a farm just south of Adamsville.

20

THE REES– GILLETT REUNIONS

AN INTERESTING aspect of the Rees family history is the Rees–Gillett Family Reunions held over a period of years from 1871 through 1923, as occasionally reported in the *Sherburne (NY) News* and the *Syracuse (NY) Daily Journal*. Also, in the later 1920's, Reese reunions were held at the Rees home by Barron Lake near Niles, Michigan.

As reported by Jason M Benton, Secretary,

A reunion of the descendants and kindred of Jacob and Annie Gillett Rees was held in the grove of Jason Benton, 1.25 miles south of Earlville, New York on Thursday, August 24, 1871. Although early morning clouds were dark and heavy, soon after 10 o'clock, friends began to assemble upon the grounds, and continued to come from east, west, north, and south. The arrival of the Midland train from Oneida (NY) brought the last of the expected guests. Happy meetings and joyous greetings were indeed the order of the day.

As the representatives of the old "Bay State" arrived, they were greeted by three rousing cheers from those already assembled. The beautiful song, "The Hills of New England" was splendidly played and sung by Mrs. Jacob (Sylvia) Rees, of Michigan, and Mrs. Warren Bush of Cortland, NY. Alfred Parsons was introduced as President of the Day, Jason Benton as Secretary, and Miles Bresee, Mrs. Alfred Parsons, and Mrs. Selden Ross as Committee of Introduction. A request was made that all present should come forward and register their names by families. The following are the names:

Otto A. Rees, Jacob J. Rees, Nancy A. Rees, Mary A. Rees, C. LeRoy Holmes, Martha L. Holmes, C.Rees Holmes, John Kinney, Sarah C. Kinney, Anna Miller, Anna Bush, Jennie Bush, Mercy A. Rees, Blennie Rees, Rebecca Rees, Albert Cole, Deville R. Rees, David C. Rees, Ellen A. Rees, Clara M. Rees, Chapel D. Rees, Nora Rees, Hascal G.C. Rees, Lovina Rees, Anna D. Rees, Frank D. Rees, Mertileo Rees, Annett Rees, Marshall Rees, Alfred Parsons, Marilla Parsons, DeForest Parsons, John R. Parsons, Jacob G. Rees, Orcelia Rees, Miller Rees, Warner Calkins, Mary R. Calkins, Livingston J. Calkins, Ellen M. Calkins, Wm. Warner Calkins, Omer H. Calkins, Simeon A. Benton, Marilla M. Benton, Simeon A. Benton, Jr., S. Anna Benton, H. Lincoln, H. Benton, C. Selden Ross, Martha L. Ross, Cora Ross, Jason M. Benton, Amelia R. Benton, Cornelia M. Benton, Lavinia R. Waldron, Elnora Moffatt, Charles Race, Wells Richmond, Caroline Richmond, Virgil Eastman, Julie Eastman, Howard Eastman, Addie Eastman, Joseph Benedict, A.L. Woodruff, L. Champlin, George H. Champlin, George Jaquius, Martha A. Jaquius, Isaac M. Bresee, Ester A. Bresee, Russel Harrington, Linus Bresee, Wally Bresee, Miles Rees,

Ellen Stoel, John Rees, Dudley L. Rees, Libbie Rees, Isaac S. Rees, William S. Rees, Knapp Rees, Fannie Rees, Morgan Houghton, Elizabeth Houghton, Mary Bassett, Martha Young, LaFayette Young, Almira Young, Albert J. Atkins, William R. Atkins, Lavantia A. Atkins, and Rachel Harrington.

At two o'clock grace was said by Rev. Mr. Gifford of Earlville and a very sumptuous dinner was served, which all present seemed to enjoy. After this Otto A. Rees gave the following history:

Jacob Rees, born March 24, 1768 and Annie Gillet, born July 14, 1773, were married January 2, 1791 in Massachusetts. They lived there until after their second child was born. Early in the year of 1795 they moved to the town of Sherburne, NY. There, eight more children were born to them. All were married in the town of Sherburne. Jacob died April 8, 1830; the mother, Annie, is still living in the town of Fabius, Onondaga County, and although too feeble to be present, 98 years of age, very familiar pictures of her were hung at each end of the table.

The names of their children: Jacob S. Rees of Michigan died in 1855; Rebecca Rees died in 1813; John M. Rees, who moved to Michigan; Martha L. Rees, also of Michigan; Simeon Gillett Rees died 1871; Otto A. Rees; Annie Rees; Mary Rees; Sarah Rees, and Caroline Rees. The descendants of Annie Gillett Rees, now living, are seven children, the youngest of which is nearly sixty years of age, 48 grandchildren, 94 great-grandchildren and five great-great-grandchildren.

The grandparents on the father's side were John Rees and Mary Spoor. The great-grandparents were Andries Rees and Rebecca Prys. The grandparents on the mother's side were Simeon Gillett and Rebecca Andrews, both born in 1744. He died January 19, 1795; she died October 6, 1826.

The families of John Rees, Isaac Rees, William Rees, Abram Rees (brothers of Jacob) were represented by their descendants, among them, beloved cousins. Also, Sarah Gillett, sister of Annie Gillett by her descendants, among them eight cousins all over fifty years of age.

After this very interesting history, a song was sung and played by Mrs. Merilla Parsons and Mrs. Helen Chapel, daughters of

Gillett Rees, entitled "Ring The Bell, Watchman."

Next in order very appropriate remarks were made by the Honorable Joseph Benedict of Utica. He said he was captivated in his early days by a Rees, and by their singing. That was Grandmother Rees, now Grandmother Bacon. She remarried in 1836, six years after Jacob died. She was one of the best Christian ladies of her time and one of the best singers God ever allowed a place in any choir. An umbrella was then shown which had been in the possession of the Rees family for more than a hundred years.

Various selected songs were sung by a large number of those present. One was, "Shall We Gather At the River?" Very interesting and appropriate remarks were then made by L. I. Caulkins of Earlville in honor his grandmother, whose picture hung directly opposite him, and which seemed to give him inspiration.

A beautiful song entitled "When Grandmama Is Gone" was sung by Miss Annie Rees of Earlville, with her father joining in the chorus.

At this time the clouds began to look threatening and thunder rolled heavily overhead. A motion was made to adjourn and to meet on August 22, 1872 in Otto Rees's dooryard. The Committee of Arrangements was reappointed—Alfred Parsons, LaFayette Young and DeWitt Rees. The company was scattered by the rain, but 68 of them met again in the evening at the home of L. I. Caulkins. Another ample repast was furnished by part of the company and a social time was passed. More songs were sung, more speeches made and recitations given. At a little past 12:00 A.M. the song, "When Shall We All Meet Again" was sung and the company then dispersed, feeling that truly this had been one of their happiest days, a day long to be remembered by all.

—Submitted by "an Eye Witness"

Although a report of the second annual reunion of the Rees–Gillett families was not found, The *Syracuse Daily Journal* contained a report of a family event which took place on July 18, 1873 in Fabius, New York. It is noted as follows.

THE CELEBRATION OF A CENTENARIAN BIRTHDAY

It is seldom that even a ripple appears upon the surface to disturb the repose of the denizens of the usually quiet village of Fabius, so pleasantly ensconced among the hills of this beautiful valley. But an event that rarely occurs more often than once in a century in the history of a community has broken the monotony and lifted the solitude, which had settled upon us.

On Monday the 14th last, Mrs. Anna Gillett Rees Bacon, for nearly 40 years a resident of this place, has attained the advanced age of one hundred years; and her living posterity, representing five generations, were assembled from all parts of our wide extended country to commemorate the event.

The gathering was one of unusual interest and all who were present felt the inspiration begotten by the occasion. Her eldest living child, now nearly eighty years of age, had come a distance of more than seven hundred miles to see his mother and mingle in the festivities of the occasion. A brother, four years his senior, died some years ago. Her remaining living children, six in number, were but a part of those present.

The arrangements were perfect, and our venerable dame was, of course, the center of attraction. No crowned head, decked with the trappings of royalty, sitting in state, surrounded by courtiers and swaying the scepter of power, ever excelled the queenly grace and dignified bearing of this venerable matron as she received the swelling tide of visitors who, for long hours, poured in and out of the apartment prepared for her reception.

Her witticisms and repartee added much to the interest of the occasion. The following is an illustration: When asked by one who came if she was feeling pretty well, she replied, "I am very well but not very pretty." Few present, however, could acquiesce in the response for it is doubtful whether any other lady of a hundred years can be found who possesses more personal attraction.

Seated at the head of several tables spread during the evening for the entertainment of her guests, she presided with all suavity and decorum for which she had been so much distinguished in her younger and palmier days.

The brief religious services were deeply interesting. They were opened by Mrs. Bacon, who sang alone the following stanzas:

"Go watch and pray, you cannot tell
How near the hour may be
And your works well done and the bell
Will toll its notes for thee.
"Death's countless snares
Beset thy way
Go, child of dust,
Go watch and pray."

Her intonation was good and her enunciation was distinct. The hymns entitled, "A Hundred Years Ago" and "A Hundred Years To Come" were then read and prayer offered. Mrs. Gillett's pastor, the Rev. Ira Clark of the Baptist Church, addressed those assembled. He recounted the important events in the moral, physical, and political history of our own and other nations during a period commencing three years before the Declaration of Independence—the time when the subject of this sketch entered upon her earthly existence—was replete with interesting incidents adapted to the occasion and listened to with close attention.

The beginning and end of a century was beautifully illustrated when this venerable mother held in her arms and pressed to her bosom, the small child of her pastor. On the whole, no event for years past in the history of our village has awakened a deeper interest or produced more food for pleasant memories and profitable contemplation.

—Signed, L. Eli Bates

THIRD ANNUAL REUNION (1873)
August 21, 1873

The third annual reunion of the Rees–Gillett families was held as usual on the old homestead grounds which were nicely fitted up by Otto A. Rees and his son Franklin with comfortable sittings, pleasant arbors, etc. The officers of the day were John Melancthon Rees of Michigan, President; Williard A. Race and Navina Benton, Vice Presidents; DeForrest Parsons, Secretary; Lafayette Young, Treasurer; O. H. Calkins, Collector, and Rush Carrier, Marshal.

The venerable and beloved centenarian, in whose honor these events have been held, about three weeks previous bid farewell to her home in Fabius, Onondaga County where she had lived nearly forty years. She came back to the old, old home in Sherburne, pictured in the previous chapter.

Her expected presence was the great attraction that brought so many together from Missouri, Indiana, Illinois, Michigan, Massachusetts, and from all parts of her own beloved state.

As the friends began to assemble on the grounds, she said to her daughter with whom she was conversing, "Let us return thanks to God for this great blessing" and called upon her eldest daughter, Mrs. Anna Miller, to pray. That prayer will be remembered by those who heard it and also the fervent responses and congratulations after which the dear old lady gave utterance to the swelling emotions of her heart.

At one o'clock the people were called to order and a very appropriate prayer was offered by Rev. D. D. Brown of the Baptist Church of Sherburne. While the names of the relatives were being registered, various songs were sung by different groups. We would be glad to speak of each separately but have only time to mention two. One, a song by three little girls of the fourth generation, Clara and Nora Rees and Mary Chapel, the youngest being only five years old. Each sustained her own part perfectly, showing that the wonderful musical talent possessed by that dear old grandmother years ago had lost none of its power as it passes from one generation to another. The other, one verse of a hymn sung by John Melancthon Reese, now seventy eight years of age. He used to sing this song with his mother in his boyhood days.

The following are the names registered in families. The total number of living descendants of the old lady is 162.

Anna Gillette Rees Bacon—100 years, one month and one week old, living in Sherburne.
Otto A. Rees, Sherburne, NY
Simeon A. Benton
Alvin G. Moses
Marilla M. Benton
Willie Fay Oakes, Guilford, NY
S. Andrew Benton
Rush W. Carrier
Hiram L. Benton
Louisa L. Carrier
J. Nevins Benton
Charley L. Carrier
Christine W. Benton
Jacob J. Rees
Charles S. Benton
Amanda Rees
John W. Benton
Mary A. Rees
Charles N. Ross
Hattie L. Rees
Mattie L. Ross
Richard L. Buell
Cora F. Ross
Mary A. Buel
Jason M. Benton
Franklin D. Buel
Cornelia M. Benton, Earlville, NY
Edith L. Buell
Simeon B. Benton, Sherburne, NY
Otto A. Buell
Andrew F. Waterman
G. LeRoy Holmes
Isabelle A. Waterman
Mattie L. Holmes
A. Fitch Waterman
Clarence R. Holmes, Sherburne, NY

Julius E. Williams
Emerette C. Thompson, Union, Michigan
Exania M. Williams, New Berlin, NY
Nancy M. Gillett
Russel H. Lee
Georgie M. Gillett, Niles, Michigan
Saphroula Lee
George W. Force
Mattie A. Foster, Sherburne, NY
Rabecca A. Force, Constantine, Michigan
John Benton
John M. Rees
Elsie A. Benton, Somerset, NY
Angeline M. Rees, Niles, Michigan
Elnora Moffett, Rome, NY
Anna Marie Nyman
Anna Mead, Pittsford, NY
Emeline Fowler, Chicago, Illinois
E. R. Brown, Ridge Road, NY
Rebecca G. Rees
Alvin Jones, Summitt, NY
Deville G. Rees
D. Carrie Richmond, New Woodstock, NY
Albert J. Cole, S. Hamilton, NY
James G. Willson, Holley, NY
Alfred Parsons
Harvey H. Moseley
S. C. M. Parsons
Mary M. Moseley
D. F. Parsons
Mattie L. Moseley
John Parsons, Earlville, NY
Harvey D. Moseley, Eaton, NY
D. A. Turner
Mary Bresee
Minnie Turner
Isaac M. Bresee

Parsons Turner, Richmond, NY
Esther A. Bresee
Dewitt C. Rees
Esther A. Bresee
Ellen A. Rees
Emma L. Bresee
Clara M. Rees
Hattie M. Bresee
Chapel D. Rees
Franklin M. Bresee
Nora M. Rees
Russell H. Bresee, Earlville, NY
Gardner Rees, S. Hamilton, NY
George H. Champlin
H. G. C. Rees
Mary L. Champlin
Lovina A. Rees
Amy L. Gray
Frank D. Rees
George C. Gray
Jacob G. Rees
Russell W. Harrington
Orselia L. Rees
Rachel M. Harrington, Rome, NY
D. M. Rees, Earlville, NY
Linus B. Bresee
Sanford L. Chapel
Wally Breese
Helen L. Chapel
Eva M. Bresee, Sherburne, NY
Mary L. Chapel
Isaac M. Rees
Walter G. Chapel, So. Hamilton, NY
Charles Rees, W. Stockbridge, MA
M. D. Rees, Waterville, NY
John Rees
Anna T. Miller, Lavonia, NY

Chapter 20—The Rees–Gillett Reunions

Isaac Rees, Chatham Village, NY
Nath C. Miller
William K. Rees, Rome, NY
Mareill E. Miller
Hart Rees
Harry D. Miller, Ft. Wayne, IN
Mrs. H. Rees, Clockville, NY
Martha L. Young
Mrs. William F. Rees, Utica, NY
Lafayette Young
A. H. Trowbridge
Almira Young
Ella A. Trowbridge, Tully, NY
Mira Young, Earlville, NY
Aurelia M. Brown
B. H. Wakely
Mary Curtis, Sherburne, NY
Martha E. Walely
Mary Curtis, Sherburne, NY
Jennie M. Bouton, McLean, NY
Joseph Benedict
William R. Atkins
Emily Benedict
Lavantia A. Atkins
Eliza Woodruff
Albert J. Atkins, Earlville, NY
Mattie Woodruff
Clinton S. Galpin
Adda Woodruff
Martha A. Galpin, Sherburne, NY
Lueretia Westcott
Warner Calkins
Nellie Westcott, Utica, NY
Mary Calkins
Bela Short
L. J. Calkins
Eliza Short, Eaton, NY

E. M. Calkins
Willard L. Race
Willie W. Calkins
Matilda Race
O. H. Calkins
Fanny W. Race
Ann R. Calkins, Earlville, NY
Lena M. Race, Oneida, NY
Caroline D. Eastman
Charles H. Race
Virgin S. Eastman
Mary A. Race
Julia E. Eastman
Walter Race, Sherburne, NY
Howard Eastman
Walter Bennett, Waterville, NY
Addie G. Eastman
Derrick Race
Willie J. Eastman, Waterville, NY
Harriet M. Race, Oxford, NY
John Kinney
M. George Sprague
Sarah Kinney, Fabius, NY
Walter R. Sprague, St. Louis, MO

At two o'clock dinner was announced and the aged mother, in her large easy chair, was moved and seated in the beautiful arbor prepared for the occasion, surrounded by her seven children, two sons and five daughters. The eldest being 78 years of age and the youngest 65.

The Brass Band of Deansville, who had discoursed sweet music at short intervals during the day, was conducted by the marshal to the front of the arbor. They played, oh so sweetly, "The Light of Other Days are Faded and Gone" after which they in turn, passed in front of her, removed their hats and bowed respectfully to her. She, with tearful eyes, returned the salutation, thus showing she did yet appreciate those tokens of respect.

Grace was said by Rev. Brown and dinner was served. Among

the beautiful things furnished for the table were some fine bouquets presented by Mrs. Jacob J. Rees, Miss Ida Owen, Mrs. W. F. Allen, Mrs. Chas. S. Waters of Sherburne, Mrs. Amy Gray of Rome, and Miss Eva Briggs of Lebanon. Also, one large pyramid cake handsomely ornamented and presented to her dear aunt by Mrs. Miles Brasee of Sherburne. Also a very elegantly decorated cake representing the Golden Age was dedicated to "Aunt Anna, born July 14, 1773" and presented to her by Mr. and Mrs. Joseph Benedict and daughter, of Utica. Time will not allow us to speak further of these beautiful things.

Dinner being over, the first cousins were called to the arbor. It was found there were twelve on the Rees side and eleven on the Gillett side, all over sixty years of age.

We were then permitted to witness one of the grandest and most beautiful sights the human eye ever rested upon. It was the clasping of hands of five successive generations, the oldest being a little past 100 years of age, and the youngest 6 years old. The interest of the scene was greatly enhanced by the presentation of a beautiful bouquet by Minnie Turner of the fifth generation to her great-great-grandmother and hearing the response of the old lady: "God bless you, my darling." Truly this was a scene that will long be remembered by all and furnished occasion for remarks by several individuals present.

The first called out was Joseph Benedict, Esq., of Utica, who responded in his own inimitable style. He said that he was proud to belong to this circle of relatives and had entertained a high respect for them from his childhood. Aunt Anna's presence brought to mind many pleasing reminiscences of his boyhood days, to some of which he made particular reference when the dear old lady responded, "I was here then, and I am here now."

Next was Melancthon Rees, the oldest living son. He was overcome with joy to meet his aged mother, sisters, brothers, and friends in this social capacity and though sad at the thought that this was perhaps the last meeting on earth with many of them, he could but rejoice at the thought that ere long they would all be gathered in that beautiful home above where partings never come.

Mr. L. J. Calkins followed with a few words to his beloved grandmother, yet could say but little as his heart was too full for utterances. The following poem was then read by its author, Ms. Amy L. Gray of Rome, NY:

When the wild and native Indians
Roamed in freedom o'er this soil
Among the first were our ancestors
To brave the danger and the toil.

This spot where we have assembled
Is where first our forefathers came.
May we ever cherish their memory
And honor their noble name.

For near a century the descendants
Have loved and hallowed this dear spot.
Time has parted them asunder
But though gone, are not forgot.

God has spared the aged mother
For a century and more.
All the forms that were familiar
To her in youth, have gone before.

Around her now are her descendants
But her companions! Where are they?
They are gone, but memory brings them
Nearer to her heart today.

This day makes our hearts so happy,
Meeting with our loved ones dear.
Oh! The many, many changes
That may come within a year.

When next reunion day you meet,
Some welcome face you may not see.
Some may be far away or gone
Dear friends, it may be you or me.

> When our reunions here are past
> And earthly friends see us no more
> May our happiest reunion be at last
> When we meet on that Golden Shore.

This was followed by a few amusing and timely remarks by Mr. H. G. C. Rees of Earlville. Then came the following short speech given by Nathaniel Miller of Indiana which seemed most fully to express the feelings of every heart present and to which all responded with a hearty "Amen."

"Friends, I suppose I may call you such, for I see here in this goodly assemblage, relatives of five generations, gathered on the old paternal sod, beneath the shadows of the old paternal roof. My grandmother, one hundred years old, and a grandchild of the fifth generation, aged six years, mingling and co-mingling in a family reunion, in social gathering with the broad blue sky above us and the green earth beneath us, and the evergreen shade shielding us from the rays of the hot August sun. If this is not enough to inspire a member of the family with enthusiasm, then I must be permitted to say it is beyond my comprehension to conceive of an event in any of our lives that would give inspiration sufficient to stir the blood to a quick flow and giving joy unbounded—joy, yes joy!

I rejoice today with joy unspeakable that I have been permitted to live to witness this event. I also rejoice that you, all my kindred, grandmother, uncles, aunts, and cousins too, are permitted to witness this event. And, yet I grieve, no, not grieve, for why should we grieve for those gone before us to a home among the blessed for eternity. Yet we can but think if it is possible, as some believe, for those in the eternal world to see and enjoy the happiness of near relatives on earth. What must be the joy, what ecstasy of bliss for Uncle Gillett Rees, Uncle Singer Rees, Urban B. Miller, my own father and Grandfather Rees, together with the others gone up there, together in a spiritual reunion in heaven looking down with joy upon this occasion. Think you not that the Father of us all does not approve these joyous gatherings and reunions? How great, grand, and glorious the thought that the time is not far distant when we all, notwithstanding the earthly separations here, shall be reunited and among that happy throng surrounding the throne, helping to swell the angelic chorus, one common brotherhood in a heavenly reunion above, with fathers, mothers, uncles, aunts, cousins, nieces, nephews, grandparents, and above all with God our Heavenly Father to dwell forevermore. May none of this goodly assemblage of relatives be left out, is my sincere prayer.

Rev. Mr. Brown was then called for. He said he was not a relative but an invited guest, and had heard so much of the old lady whom he most beautifully addressed as Queen of the day, and knew so many of the friends so well, he felt he had a right to claim a part relationship, at least, and felt the same inspiration breathed into his heart which had seemed to fill every soul present. He felt he had to thank God he had lived to see this day.

Various other speeches were made and songs were sung and all the older ones joined in one grand chorus, "All Hail the Power of Jesus' Name." After this, all present sang "Shall We Gather At the River." This song brought fresh to all our minds that one we loved and was with us one year ago, Mrs. Boughton of Massachusetts, had passed over the river and was, we doubt not, with the others of whom previous mention has been made, rejoicing over this reunion.

The following persons were appointed as a committee of arrangements for the ensuing year: Rush W. Carrier, DeWitt C. Rees, Nevina Benton, Miles Brasee, William Atkins, Jacob C. Rees, Derrick Race, Nathaniel Miller and Jacob J. Rees.

A unanimous vote of thanks was given the Deansville Brass Band for their gentlemanly deportment as well as fine selections of music and admirable execution. One piece is particularly worthy of note, not only for the soft and sweet style of execution, but also for its particular adaptation to the times. That is the soul inspiring air, "Home Sweet Home." It always rouses the dormant feelings of every soul and calms even the savage breast to peace with its sweet strains of home.

The meeting was adjourned to meet on the same grounds, Thursday, August 20, 1874.   —Signed, Ellen M. Calkins

The Sherburne News of Saturday September 5, 1874 published an extensive report on the Rees and Gillett reunion as follows.

FOURTH ANNUAL REUNION (1874)
August 20, 1874

The relatives and descendants of the Rees and Gillett families held their Fourth Annual Picnic on Thursday, August 20, 1874, on the "Old Homestead" grounds. Everything connected therewith was arranged in fine order by Otto A. Rees and his son Franklin, as usual. The splendid evergreen grove in front of the house was prepared with a platform, seats, swing, croquet grounds, etc., in such manner as would be calculated to be comfortable for the old, pleasant for the middle aged, and amusing for the young.

The officers on duty for the day were: Otto A. Rees, President; Philip G. Gillett, L.L.D. and Derrick Race, Vice Presidents; J. Nevins Benton, Secretary; Miles Bresee, Treasurer; Willard L. Race, Collector; and Rush W. Carrier, Marshal.

In the earlier part of the day the clouds looked dark and portentous, but as the day wore on the sky presented a more favorable aspect, and at the hour of noon all fears of an inclement day were dispelled. The friends then congratulated themselves that a more beautiful time for the occasion could not have been selected.

The morning express train from the south, arriving between 8 and 9 o'clock, brought upwards of twenty guests from Green, Oxford and other stations, and were promptly conveyed to the grounds by the village liveries, private carriages, etc. The 10 ½ morning express from the north came in with about 30 friends aboard, from Utica, Watersville, Deansville, and intermediate points, besides Beers Brass Band of Deansville being on the train. This last delegation was immediately conducted to the "Promised Land" by the Marshal, R. W. Carrier, headed by the Brass Band and arriving on the grounds at 11 o'clock. In addition to these, private conveyances filled with cousins, uncles, aunts, parents and children, old and young, came from various points, until by 12 o'clock over two hundred persons might have been seen on the grounds.

Previous to the time of one o'clock the hour was spent in salutations, greeting of friends long parted, and various other ways. The most prominent feature of attraction, however, about this time was "Aunt Anna" who not being able to occupy her place in the arbor, received her many friends in her room in the central part of the house. Although her mental faculties have become somewhat impaired since a year ago, still physically Father Time has dealt very gently with her and she seemed to enjoy the congratulations and her extensive circle of relatives, and in a particularly marked degree, appreciated the occasion.

Another object of curiosity was a "Genealogy of the Gillett Family," by the Rev. S. T. Gillett, D.D. of Indianapolis, Indiana. It was conspicuously displayed upon one of the largest trees in the grove, and a large group gathered about while it was being explained by its author. The swing and croquet grounds were well occupied all this time by the younger portion of the company and the Brass Band, at short intervals, was discoursing sweet music to all.

At 1 o'clock the friends were called to order by the President and the Throne of Grace was invoked by Rev. S. T. Gillett, D.D., Presiding Elder of the M.E. Conference of Central Indiana. After music by the band, the Honorable Joseph Benedict of Utica was called to the stand and in a brief but appropriate speech alluded to the departed ones of our circle who were at our last reunion one year ago.

He first spoke of the lamented Livingston J. Calkins of Earlvillle, who died December 5, 1873. Truly do we miss him, as he was one of the originators of these reunions and always acted a prominent part at each gathering. The next death reported was that of Miss Mattie Mosely, daughter of Harvey H. Mosely of Eaton, which occurred January 24, 1874, "taken in the bloom of youth." The third death among our number was Amelia R. Benton, wife of Jason M. Benton of Earlville who died June 7, 1874. It may well be that "None knew her but to love her." The last deceased relative who was with us in 1873 was Mrs. Harriet M. Race, wife of Derrick Race of Oxford. She died June 23, 1874. Mr. Benedict paid fitting tributes of respect to each of the departed friends and seemed to feel, in an eminent degree, the great loss we have all sustained, and though his remarks were brief, they were full of sympathy for our afflicted friends. In conclusion, he exhorted all to "hold in grateful remembrance and sacredly cherish the memories of our dear ones who have passed over the river and strive to imitate their virtues, stimulated by the hope that we shall all one day meet in the happy reunion above."

Following these eulogies an appropriate dirge was played by the band. Immediately thereafter Mrs. Amy L. Gray of Rome, NY was introduced and read the following original poem.

> Amid these scenes of joy and pleasure
> Friends and kindred meet at last;
> Some with joy and some with sorrow
> Note the changes of the past.
>
> There are many of our loved ones
> That have met with us before;
> That will never gather with us
> Till we meet on that bright shore.
>
> But life is but a changing dream
> We meet on earth to part again;
> We realize our fondest hopes
> To find, alas, that all is vain!
>
> As year by year glides swiftly by
> All that have gathered here today;
> Must grasp death's cold and icy hand.
> One by one we must pass away.
>
> Let us, as we journey onward,
> Each and all for death prepare;

That we may join that happy number
That shall gather over there.

Let us prize this happy meeting
With the aged mother once again.
Soon she'll join those gone before her
But our loss will be her gain.

May the bonds of love again unite
Our hearts in heaven as on earth below;
No farewell there! But a song of praise
For parting there, we shall not know.

And when we meet beyond the river
On that bright and golden shore;
That will be our last reunion—
We shall meet to part no more.

Next came the following amusing "Historical Poem" concerning Jacob Rees and family and their settlement in Sherburne in 1794. It was written by S. B. Marsh, Esq., of Albany, NY, a particular friend of the family in his younger days. It was read by Joseph Benedict, Esq., as follows.

In olden times and years gone by,
When love or money could not buy
The common luxuries now enjoyed
By honest people well employed,
'Twas then and here on his home ground
My theme begins! For here was found
A place well suited for to please
Both JACOB and SWEET ANNA REES.
In seventeen hundred ninety-four
He left West Stockbridge to explore
The western world, and find a place
For him and his rising race.
He was directed to this spot;

And here he chose to cast his lot.
The trees were thick and large and tall
Yet he decreed that they should fall.
The first years struggle all alone
Secured an opening for a home.
One acre cleared—a house prepared,
The best the town could then afford.
A log house it was made tight and warm,
Secure from danger and all harm;
The latch-string out! when 'twas not in,
For Jacob meant to live therein.
So to his family he went
To bring them here was his intent;
In seventeen hundred and ninety-five
They here in safety did arrive.
'Twas here SWEET ANNA found a home
Tho' often by herself alone;
No one to bid her heart good cheer
Save Jacob and two children dear.
'Twas hers to act a noble part
So that in life might get a start
That in the years to come should prove
To make their home a home of love,
Health, strength and courage was their boon.
And they were bent to see how soon
A clearing they could make and raise
Some food for coming winter days.
'Twas on this wise
The sunny skies
Peeked in among the trees.
For clearing made,
Removed the shade
And let in sun and breeze.
For some few years
Through many fears
Did Jacob struggle well.
Unceasing toil

Laid bare the soil
And heavy blows began to tell!
The country new
The neighbors few
'Twas often that they sought to spend
(With children, too,
Through storm and whew-)
A winter evening with a friend.
The ox and sled
Were often made
The way of traveling through the woods;
Pole in! The way
On straw and hay,
In overcoats and winter hoods!
The whip was long
The team was strong
The bells were placed on board;
Whoever dare
With proper care,
Might ring them on the road.
At nine o'clock
'Twas all the talk
To start – their team was slow!
But what a sight!
Old Buck and Bright
Went trotting through the snow!
The farm was cleared
The boys were reared
To work and plan like men;
Sweet Anna too,
Taught the girls to sew
On dresses fine and plain;
For she could always work and sing
And make the best of everything;
And happy in her days employ
Infused and filled each heart with joy.

But father Jacob had a rule
That all of his must go to school;
So he contrived a pung to carry
Jacob, Rebecca, Gillett, and Martha;
Malencthon, too, was on and off
As snow banks proved both hard and soft.

The nearest school was in the Quarter;
A school of yore, taught by a master;
Here pung and pony—children too,
Remained each day 'til school was through
Then all on board, they did sing out some!
Whip up! And go for happy home.

These days and times have passed away;
A very few that's here today,
May call to mind these day school scenes;
But more they seem like by-gone dreams,
Yet, of the past, the bitter and the sweet,
'Tis good to think! For this we meet
Some precious promise of eternal love
Bestowed in kindness from above.

I saw kind ANNA, first, in eighteen six,
Perhaps the time, just now, I cannot fix;
But sure I am 'twas there about,
And I will tell how it came out.
She came to church where I did sing,
And kindly took me 'neath her wing;
For I sung counter with the women,
And that set all the people grinning!
Kind ANNA sung the counter too;
In her I found good help, and new;
For I had sung alone one day,
And had it all in my own way!
Now she was very kind,
And took me by her side,

And taught me many things
That stirred my childish pride.
For in the good old tunes of yore
The parts all strove to get before;
And some there were, the very worst,
That each part tried to get out first.
But this kind ANNA was so true
In singing tunes, both old and new,
That all admired her, justly too,
For it was plain what she could do.

She was, in truth, the singer of that day,
For this is what the people, all, did say;
On all occasions, public, she was there
To sing the counter, tenor, or the air.
Her songs were of the puritan kind,
That cheered the heart, directed the mind
To themes so rapturous and mysterious
Even angels bowed and were desirous
To know the wonders of redemption,
By Jesus Christ, the souls salvation!

Such themes so cheering
Wak'd up much feeling
Young and old began to sing!
The log house rang
When they all sang
Sweet songs to Christ their King!
These offerings were not vain;
God heard and answered prayer.
In early life their children learned
To cast on Christ their care.
Ten children used to meet
Around their father's board,
And there discourse on passing scenes
And thank and praise the Lord.
Near all their names were Bible names,

Reminding us of ancient times.
Jacob, Rebecca, John and Martha,
Simeon, Anna, Mary and Sarah;
The other two I cannot tell
What their initials might not spell;
Otto A. and Caroline D.,
I do not know what they might be,
But sure I am their life appears
As fair as any of their years.
And now this record stands alone!
Its equal I have never known!
Names of the ancients we revere,
Admire their faith—their God we fear.
Alas! This record has been broke!
The father and three children gone!
Death has invaded this dear group
And laid them in the silent tomb!
The rest are here this festal day
To greet each other on their way
Through earth and cares to that blessed home
Where sin and death can never come!

They're also here to greet their mother,
Whose sainted form and patriarchal view
Commands respect and love and kindest care
That she, the woes of life, may better bear.

Of her, I wish once more to speak
And then I close. I only seek
To tell of duties she has done;
The Master served—the victor won!

In passing years when God came near to bless
His Word and cause and give them great success,
'Twas then Aunt Anna raised her voice in song
Among a weeping multitude and throng.

When anxious sinners heard her words of praise
They sought to join with her in these sweet lays,
Which sing of Christ, who came from heaven above
To prove His Godhead, and His wondrous love!

Her faith in her baptismal rite was shown,
For first she was to lead the people down
Nearby the waters edge; while her sweet voice
Broke forth in song and bid them all rejoice.

In solemn meeting too she bore her part,
And seemed to give the blessed work her heart,
And voice and strength and time, even everything
That sinners might be saved through Christ, our King.
And thus she was first in this great work of grace,
To encourage saints and save the fallen race;
And by her faith and works and zeal she has proved
Her interest in Jehovah's well beloved.

And now she has lived for many years and seen
How good and kind to her the Lord has been;
Around five generations come this day
To greet Aunt Anna, and with reverence pay
Their thanks to God for His preserving care
Of her whose life to us is precious, rare!
Yet we are conscious she has almost done
With earth, and waiting for her heavenly home!

Goodbye Aunt Anna, we will leave thee here,
And hope to see you at this time next year;
But should the Master call thee, all is well!
The song that never ends, you'll help to swell!

At the conclusion of Mr. Marsh's poem, the Deansville Band enlivened the friends again with a national air. A short time was then devoted to registering the names of the relatives present, by families, the heads of families being in capitals, and the postal address of the different members listed. The list of names reported runs thus:

ANNA BACON, aged 1 century, 1 year, 1 month, 1 week, of Sherburne, NY

Otto A. Rees, Sherburne, NY; Alvin G. Moses; Carrie A. Moses, Guilford, NY; Rush W. Carrier; Louisa L. Carrier; Charley L. Carrier, Sherburne, NY; Jacob J. Rees; Amanda Rees; Mary A. Rees; Hattie L. Rees, Sherburne, NY; Richard L. Buell; Mary A. Buell; Flora L. Buell; Franklin D. Buell; Edith L. Buell; Otto A. Buell; David C. Buell; C. LeRoy Holmes; Mattie L. Holmes; Clarence R. Holmes, Sherburne, NY; Rebecca G. Rees; Devillo Rees; Albert J. Cole, South Hamilton, NY; Alfred Parsons; S. C. Marilla Parsons; Prof. P. G. Gillett, L.L.D., Jacksonville, IL; Anna Mead; Edmund R. Brown, Ridge Road, NY; Alvin Jones, Summit, NY; Mrs. J. R. Rees; Blendena Rees, Edwardsburg, MI; James G. Wilson, Holley, NY; Bella Short; Mary M. Moseley, Eaton, NY; Estellus Smith; Frances A. Smith; Lewis S. Smith; Eugene Smith; Estellus Smith, Jr.; Walter Smith; Frances May Smith, Hamilton, NY; Mrs. R.W.Richmond; H. S. Gorton, New Woodstock, NY; Nancy N. DeClercq, Cazenovia, NY; N. Ackley; Nancey G. Ackley, Albany, NY; DeForest Parsons; John Parsons, Earlville, NY; DeWitt C. Rees; Ellen A. Rees; Clara M. Rees; Chapel D. Rees; Nora M. Rees; Gardner Rees, South Hamilton, NY; H. G. C. Rees; Lovina A. Rees; Anna D. Rees; Frank D. Rees, Hamilton, NY; Orselia L. Rees; D. Miller Rees, Earlville, NY; Sanford L. Chapel; Helen M. Chapel; Mary L. Chapel; Walter G. Chapel, South Hamilton, NY; Marshall D. Rees, Earlville, NY; Anna T. Miller, Savona, NY; Warren S. Bush; Anna M. Bush; Jennie Bush, Cortland, NY; Rev. G.A. Simonson; George M. Simonson, Newark, NJ, Martha L. Young, LaFayette Young, Almira Young, Mira Young, Earlville, NY; William R. Atkins; Lavantia A. Atkins; Albert J. Atkins, Earlville, NY; Clinton S. Galpin; Martha A. Galpin, Sherburne, NY; Ellen M. Calkins; Willie W. Calkins; Omar H. Calkins; Ann R. Calkins, Earlville, NY; Virgil S. Eastman; Julia E. Eastman; Howard Eastman; Addie G. Eastman, Waterville,

NY; Joseph Benedict; Emity Benedict; Mattie Woodruff; Adda Woodruff; Lucretia Westcott; Nellie Westcott, Utica, NY; Mary Bresee; Isaac M. Bresee; Esther A. Bresee; Emma L. Bresee; Hattie M. Bresee; Franklin M. Bresee; Russell H. Bresee; Rees Bresee, Earlville, NY; George H. Champlin, Amy L. Gray, Rome, NY; Russell W. Harrington; Rachel M. Harrington; Linus S. Bresee; Waity R. Bresee; Eva M. Bresee, Sherburne, NY; Mrs. D. C. Bresee, Binghamton, NY; Cornelia N. Sperring, Oxford, NY; Mary A. Willoughby, South Oxford, NY; Dwight Curtiss; Mary A. Curtiss; Lydia R. Curtiss; Clara L. Curtiss, Sherburne, NY; Willard L. Race; Matilda Race; Fanny W. Race; Lena M. Race, Oneida, NY; Charles H. Race; Mary A. Race; Walter Race, Sherburne, NY; John Bennett; Walter J. Bennett; Anna Bennett; Lynn Bennett, Waterville, NY; Derrick Race; Sarah A. Root, Oxford, NY; Alvin Race; Jennie L. Race, Watertown, NY; Austin W. Race; Sarah E. Race; N.B. Race; John Kinney; Sarah C. Kinney, Fabius, NY; Frank L. Verdenberg, Geneva, NY; Amos Fleming; Carrie Fleming, Geneva, NY; Simeon A. Benton; Marilla M. Benton; S. Andrew Benton; S. Anna Benton; Hiram Lynn Benton; Fred A. Benton; J. Nivins Benton; Christine W. Benton; Charley S. Benton; John W. Benton; C. Selden Ross; Mattie L. Ross; Cora F. Ross; Jason M. Benton; Cornelia M. Benton, Earlville, NY; Betsey Benton; Stephen B. Benton, Sherburne, NY; Andrew F. Waterman; Isabelle A. Waterman; A. Fitch Waterman, New Berlin, NY; Russell H. Lee; Sophronia Lee, Sherburne, NY; William E. Higgs; Alice L. Higgs; Thomas E. Higgs, Utica, NY; Lenora Moffett, Rome, NY; Rev. Samuel T. Gillett, D.D.; Harriet A. Gillett, Indianapolis, IN; George Race; Mary L. Race; Richard E. Race; Nicholas Race; Mary P. Race; Frankie W. Race, Brisban, Chenango County, NY; Derrick Race; Catherine M. Race; John Benedict; Hannah M. Benedict; Joseph A. Wheeler, Greene, NY; Ethan Race; Martha A. Race; Ernest Race, Greene, NY; Maria B. Fish; Mary Carpenter, Utica, NY; William G. Young; Polly W. Young; Julia A. Buckley; George A. Young; Emma J. Young; O. J. Hart; Laura H. Hart; Florence A. Hart; Sylvia St. John Whitney; Jerod Whitney;

Mary E. Whitney; Samuel Whitney; Nancy Whitney, Deansville, NY; Anna W. Peck; Seth W. Peck, Marshall B. Peck, Marshall, NY.

At this time, the hour of 2 o'clock having arrived, the president announced that the friends would occupy seats around the bountifully loaded and tastefully arranged dinner table. This suggestion was promptly obeyed by the "anxious family" and the table was quickly surrounded. Thanks was returned by Rev. G.A. Simonson of Newark, New Jersey, and the people were soon partaking of a "feast of good things."

We would not fail to speak, in this connection, of several fine bouquets which were ornamenting the table, presented by Miss Eva Bresee, Mrs. C. Galpin, Mrs. Clara Curtiss and Mrs. C. S. Waters of Sherburne; Mrs. William Rhodes of Earlville; Mrs. Amy L. Gray of Rome and Miss Jennie Bush of Cortland; also a beautiful "evergreen cross" with a hanging flower basket underneath, presented by Mrs. Rachel M. Harrington of Sherburne; and a large and beautifully ornamented fancy cake surrounded by silver gilt leaves and mounted with raised flowers, bearing the inscription "To Aunt Anna 100+1, 1874," and presented to the old lady by the Hon. Joseph Benedict and family of Utica. It was much admired.

Directly after dinner, by request, Professor Phillip G. Gillett of Jacksonville, Illinois took the president's chair, and after music by the band, introduced Rev. G.A. Simonson as the first speaker. He felt proud to belong to the Rees and Gillett families, having married a granddaughter of the old lady. He assured the friends the numerous greetings and social friendships with which he had been initiated into this group of cousins at this, the first visit at the reunions, would always remain a "bright spot" in all his future years.

The Rev. J. N. Tolman of Woodstock was next invited to come forward. He accepted the invitation, took the stand and remarked that "although not a relative of this great family" that he had been intimately acquainted with the old lady for a long time. For several years he had officiated as her pastor at Fabious,

NY and unhesitatingly asserted that "she was one of the best Christian women he ever knew."

Next came Joseph Benedict who made a few remarks concerning his early life, courtship and connection with the Rees family, bringing to mind, he said, many happy recollections of his early life, by meeting dear Aunt Anna.

After listening to more cheering music by the band, Rev. S. T. Gillett was introduced as "one of the best of fathers" by his son, the acting president. Mr. Gillett, who by the way is now visiting the home of his youth in company with his estimable lady for the first time in twenty-two years, now came forward and occupied the stand. He prefaced his remarks by saying that his heart was full of joy at meeting such a large company of his kindred, most of them for the first time in his life; and particularly alluded to "our dear aunt, whose form is still with us," in terms of the greatest respect and reverence. He then gave a short account of his early life in following the high seas; his return home and subsequent conversion, dating from that time of his determination to enter the ministry. He stated that with his Bible and Methodist hymn book he started out to preach the Gospel, and that he had not been kept from the pulpit ten Sabbaths in the past thirty-seven years on account of ill health. He closed with an earnest and effecting exhortation to his relatives present to meet him finally in that "bright home in heaven." His remarks found a ready response in many hearts, a large number being moved to tears.

At this point in the exercises, many present desired to hear from Professor Phillip G. Gillett, son of the last speaker. When he took the stand, he pleasantly alluded to the gratification of mingling for the first time with so extensive a circle of friends connected by ties of consenguinity but confessed that he experienced some difficulty in unraveling the intricate chain of relationship into which he had been initiated during the fore part of the day. After paying his respects to his dear aunt, in terms of commendation, he proceeded to speak of the natural benefits arising from an association of friends in these social capacities; of the influence we have upon, and the duties we owe to each other, and enlarged upon the importance of a liberal, practical education in order to properly discharge the responsibilities of the age. But we would not attempt to give a synopsis of the masterly speech of Prof. Gillett. Suffice it to say, it was listened to with respectful attention throughout, the speaker being frequently applauded.

The Deansville Brass Band delightfully entertained us with another beautiful selection. Then Rev. S. T. Gillett read a genealogy of the Gillett family, of his own production, dating back upwards of one-hundred and fifty years and bringing it down to the present time; furnishing much interesting information and many valuable statistics. After this, upon invitation, Ira Crane, Esq. of Earlville, made a few pertinent remarks, mainly referring to the aged matron whom this day delights to honor and who "had been a true Christian lady for over eighty years."

Mr. H. G. C. Rees of Hamilton indulged in a few earnest remarks, in his own inimitable style, followed by a short and humorous speech by Prof. W. L. Race, principal of Oneida Academy, Oneida, NY.

Otto A. Rees then gave a brief but interesting history concerning the immigration of his parents to this town; their settlement on the old homestead; their labors and hardships connected with their clearing the forests, cultivating the soil and obtaining a competency for themselves and family during the earlier years of their pioneer life.

After this the friends joined in singing the beautiful song, "Shall We Gather At The River." This brought to mind one whose voice was prominent in singing this song a year ago, L. Calkins of Earlville, who we trust has been gathered with the saints at the river.

We would not omit to record another genealogy of the Gillett family, for the originality of which we are indebted to Mr. Otto A. Rees who has succeeded in obtaining a distinct chain through ten generations; five previous to the date of Anna Gillett's birth and five since then. It was read by Prof. P. G. Gillett and runs as follows.

Jonathan Gillett and his brother Nathan emigrated from England to America and first settled in Dorchester, MA in 1630. His wife's name does not appear. He had a son Jonathan Gillett, Jr., born in Dorchester, date unknown. He married Mary Relay of Hartford, CT, the 23rd of April 1661. She died April 18, 1676. He was married again Dec. 14, 1676 to Miriam Dibble. They had a son, Thomas Gillett, born in Windsor, CT, May 31, 1678. Thomas was married Nov. 21, 1700 to Martha Mills; she died and he married Hannah Clarke on Feb. 26, 1704. They had a son, Jonah Gillett, born Oct. 18, 1708 and he married Mary Lewis on Dec. 17, 1731. They had a son, Simeon Gillett, born in Wintonburg, now Bloomfield, Connecticut on Oct. 16, 1743 and was married to Rebecca Andrews on May 20, 1762. They had six or seven children, one of whom is Anna Gillett.

Anna Gillett was born July 14, 1773 and she is my mother and belongs to the sixth generation, her children to the seventh, her grandchildren to the eighth, her great-grandchildren to the ninth and her great-great-grandchildren to the tenth generation.

Mrs. Marilla Parsons of Earlville, Mrs. Anna Miller of Savona, NY and Mrs. S. T. Gillett of Indianapolis, IN responded to an invitation for the ladies to speak, each indulging in brief remarks pertaining to this pleasant reunion of friends, the latter of whom being introduced by her son, Professor Gillett as "one of the best mothers." By her unassuming manner and pleasing address she convinced all that the title was worthily bestowed.

At the request of many friends, Prof. P. G. Gillett now came forward and gave some instruction in the "Deaf and Dumb" language, which was a rare entertainment to all, particularly the rendering of the Lord's Prayer which was extremely beautiful. We might mention in this connection that Prof. Gillett has for the past eighteen years occupied the responsible and honorable position of principal of the Deaf and Dumb Institute of Illinois, located in Jacksonville.

Mrs. A. Parsons, Mrs. Helen Chapel, Mrs. Anna Bush and a few others then sang, "A Hundred Years To Come," producing a profound impression. A formal dismissal of the Brass Band, in behalf of the relatives, was then given by the president, thanking them for the fine selection of music and the admirable execution of the same. Also, the thanks of the audience was tendered to Otto A. Rees and son for their efforts in contributing to the comfort and convenience of guests in the fine arrangement of the picnic. We would also mention the token remembrance displayed by Edmund R. Brown, Esq. In presenting to dear Aunt Anna, a quantity of luscious peaches, being a sample of the produce of his twenty acre peach orchard located on the well-known "Ridge Road" near Lockport, NY.

On motion, the following persons were unanimously chosen a committee of arrangement for the ensuing year: Alfred Parsons, Miles Bresee, LaFayette Young, Andrew Benton, O. H. Calkins, William G. Young, and Charles H. Race. The assembly then adjourned to meet on the same grounds Thursday, August 19, 1875.

—J. Nevins Benton, Secretary

AUTHOR'S NOTE: Although the reunions have continued on each year, newspaper reports have not been kept by the families contacted. Aunt Anna Gillett Rees passed away October 2, 1875 at the age of 102—six weeks after the fifth reunion. Missing newspaper stories may be available in libraries in The Syracuse–Utica–Sherburne area. It is also possible the picture album mentioned in the following account may have been placed in a local library.

A report of the 34TH ANNUAL PICNIC of the "Reese–Gillette Families" (note the spellings), in the *Syracuse Daily Journal* was in the form of a letter to Aunt Mary Rees Calkins of 11 Aiken Street, Utica, NY from John Reese Parsons of Earlville, NY, August 25, 1904.

> My Dear Aunt Mary:
> Your nieces and nephews, to the number of 64, assembled yesterday for their 34th annual picnic at the spacious old fashioned home of the Bresee family, two miles south of Earlville. You know it as an ideal spot for a family picnic, and you easily recall its quaint old-time fireplaces, wide doorways, large rooms, the nice lawn, the old schoolhouse nearby, the little park and the beautiful flowing Chenango River. Then too, it is sort of Baptist ground. You remember the many times you have stood near the old bridge to see the ordinance of baptism administered to new members of the Earlville Baptist Church. It was at the old Bresee home where they were always taken to rearrange their clothing. Our family has always been a power in the Baptist church, so it was our "meet and bounden duty" to assemble at that place this year. Esther Bresee and her daughter Hattie, occupy one side of the house and her son Russell H. and his wife, the other side. They made it very pleasant for us and we had an enjoyable day. There were no speeches this year, but we all sat together for a good old visit. All regretted that you could not be there and

many kind inquiries were made as to your welfare.

Cousin Eliza Thompson of Union, Michigan reported the death of her son-in-law Harvey Hitchcock, the death of Martha Collins and Kendrick B. Miller, all of whom you have seen and remember. She also said Cousin Anna Nyman of Chicago had been helpless and speechless for 2 years as a result of paralysis.

Since our last picnic Mr. Fred Benton and Miss Hattie Bresee have collected the printed reports of each year's picnic and put them neatly into a scrapbook along with many pictures of persons and picnic groups. This book is to be preserved and brought to the picnic every year. I have a photograph of your mother when she was 96 years old and will put that in with the others.

We named for next year's officers: Linn S. Chapel, President; Alfred Reese, Vice President; Hattie M. Bresee, Secretary; Committeee of Arrangements, S. Gillett Reese, Chairman and R. H. Bresee and Fred Benton.

Your own family was represented by Eilen M. Robinson, Minnie L. Calkins, Ray and Paul Calkins.

Otto's family showed Mary Buell, Levi Collins, Edith Collins, Earl Buell, Levisa Carrier, Harriet Carrier, Rush Carrier, L.C. and Martha Holmes.

Caroline's household sent Virgil Eastman, Howard Flora, Florence and Mary Eastman. Martha's house had but a single delegate in the person of Almira Young.

Simeon Gillett's descendants present were: Myrteloo J. Reese, Nettie Reese, Marshall D. Reese, Mrs. M. D. Reese, Dr. and Mrs. John Greene, Stanley and Otto Greene, Mr. and Mrs. J. D. Holey, S. Gillette Reese, Della and Lucy Orcelia Reese, Viola Reese, Alfred P., Lennie M. and Leslie A. Reese, John Reese Parsons, Ola, Rilla, Una and Fred C. Parsons, Clara Collins, Perry, Nina, Clinton and Louise Collins.

Deacon Simeon Benton's family showed S. Andrew Benton, Fred and Minnie Benton, C. S. and Martha Ross, Cornelia and Marjorie Bergan.

The Bresees present were Esther M., Hattie M. Russell, H., Eva L. and Ray Bresee, Emerton and Esther Wilcox. Charles Race was the sole delegate from the Race family.

As visitors we had Viola Baker, Odessa Brown, and Maxon Sturgess Crumb.

One cousin facetiously remarked, "The cousins present remind me of a visit to the woods near my boyhood home. I saw there a few old familiar trees, some broken stubs and decaying stumps, but most of the ground was occupied by the young second growth timber." The children did seem to be all there this year.

Virgil Eastman brought some of last years apples, which were in a good state of preservation. Cousin Mary Buell lost a very nice sponge cake somewhere around the house, but the committee found it for the president of the day, Howard S. Eastman. Fred Parsons came with his camera and got a very nice photograph of the entire company.

As you will soon pass your 99th birthday anniversary, it is the hearty wish of all your kindred that you may be permitted to round out a century of life with every faculty as bright as it is now.

Your nephew,
John Reese Parsons

REES–GILLETT PICNIC (1906)

Thursday, August 23, 1906 at the home of S. Gillett Rees occurred the 36th annual reunion of the Rees–Gillett cousins. Fifty-five of the cousins were present and spent a most enjoyable day.

Cousin LeRoy Holmes extended an invitation to the cousins to hold the reunion at his home next year. The invitation was gladly accepted and it is hoped a large number may be present. Let us all decide now to be present at the reunion next year, if possible. Cousin LeRoy has been very faithful for the past 36 years. He has never missed a reunion.

During the year Aunt Mary Calkins and Cousin Rachel M. Harrington have passed beyond. Aunt Mary lived to be nearly 100 years old and had kept all her faculties until her death. She was the last one of her generation.

In looking over reports of former picnics, special mention has been made of the good dinner served. Those who were present this year will be willing to testify that the art of cooking is not a lost art in the Rees-Gillett family. The dinner this year was especially well prepared. The table fairly groaned with good things. The only thing lacking was one of Aunt Rebecca's chicken pies.

Dr. Rees, president of the day, being absent, Russell Bresee took charge of the business of the day. The following officers for next year were chosen and elected. President, Russell H. Bresee; Vice President, J. G. Rees; Committee of Arrangements, Jerry Holey, J. R. Parsons and S. Gillett Rees.

Cousins in attendance were Andrew Benton, Seldon Ross, Martha Ross, Margery Bergan, LeRoy Holmes, Mate Buell, Edith Collins, Earl Collins, Levisa Carrier, Sanford Chapel, Artie Chapel, Carrie Chapel, Jerry Holey, Mary Holey, Charlie Collins, Clara Collins, Nina Collins, Perry Collins, Clinton Collins, Louise Collins, Ellen Robinson, Ray Calkins, Viola Parsons, Ola Parsons, Rilla Parsons, Una Parsons, Jacob G. Rees, Nettie Rees, Viola Rees, Viola Baker, Gillett Rees, Della Rees, Orcelia Rees, Elizabeth Rees, Alfred Rees, Lina Rees, Leslie Rees, Rachel Rees, Nora Usher, Robert Usher, Marshal Rees, Carol Brown, Esther Bresee, Harriet M. Bresee, H. Ray Bresee, Etta Wilcox, Emmerton Wilcox, Russell Bresee, Eva Bresee, S. D. Dutton, Chloe Bresee Dutton, Mary Dutton Hyde, Neil Hyde and Addie Calkins. Visitor present was Florence Conant.

—Secretary of the Day

40TH ANNUAL REES–GILLETT PICNIC (1910)

The 40th annual Rees–Gillett picnic was held August 18, 1910 at the Stone Lodge Farm, the home of Mr. and Mrs. Davis Oliver. There were present 63 of the cousins and with bounteous luncheons brought by them, together with the previous arrangements made, such as games, swings, etc., a very enjoyable day was spent by this old family. After the repast was served, the people assembled in a large tent erected on the lawn for the purpose. Songs were sung and short speeches were made after being called to order by the president of the day, Mr. Ray Calkins of Cincinnatus, NY.

At the end of the speeches the following officers were elected for the ensuing year: President, Andrew Benton; Vice President, Frank Benton; Secretary, Fred Benton; Executive Committee, Gilett Rees, Russell Bresee and Arthur Chapel.

Letters were read from those cousins who were unable to attend the picnic. A pleasant time visiting followed, together with an automobile ride for the few who had never ridden in a machine before. When the party began to break up, they all decided that they had spent a very pleasant day and hoped that all and more would meet next year at the home of Mr. Andrew Benton.

THE 47TH ANNUAL REUNION (1917)

The 47th annual Reese–Gillette Family Reunion was held at the residence of J. D. Holey on August 30, 1917. The day was cold and rainy with only 45 cousins present, but the hospitality of the host and hostess put all in good cheer and a grand visit was enjoyed. Charles W. Carrier, as president of the day, drew out some entertaining remarks from all the talkers in the family and the talkless ones indulged in patriotic songs related to the war.

From out of town there were: Rev. Kendrick Benton of Chicago; Attorney William Benton of Saratoga, NY; Dr. F. E. Reese with Byron Widger and family of Cortland and Harriet Bresee of Atlantic City.

In past years cousins have come to the picnic in all manner of conveyances from ox-carts to autos. One tried to convince the cousins he came this year in a balloon, but he could not show us the balloon. He was voted into the Ananias Club. The officers for next year are Mrs. J. D. Holey, president and Ola P. Crandall, Secretary.

48TH REESE–GILLETTE REUNION (1918)

The 48th annual Reese–Gillette Family Reunion was held at the home of Mr. and Mrs. Will Usher of East Hamilton on Thursday, August 29, 1918. There were 35 cousins present from New York, Atlantic City, Waterville, Deansboro, Sherburne, Cortland, Earlville, Norwich and Hubbardsville. Letters were read from cousins Anna Race of Buffalo and Carrie L. Reese of Rome, NY. LeRoy Holmes who has attended every reunion and Mrs. Esther Bresee who has attended 47, were present and recognized.

Interesting topics of the day were discussed by Dr. F. D. Reese, Charles Carrier, J. R. Parsons, Rev. Lewis, Harriet and others as called upon by the president of the day, Mrs. Mary Holey. The deaths of Mrs. D. S. Parsons and S. L. Chapel were reported and flowers were sent to Mrs. Charles Humphrey, Sherburne and Mrs. Linn Chapel of Elmira.

Eight young cousins were reported as engaged in the service of their country: Earl Collins, Daniel Eastman, Clinton Collins and the five Green boys—Nelson, Harold, Stanley, Otto, and John.

The following officers were elected for next year: President, Miss Harriet Bresee, and Secretary, Miss Una M. Parsons. After an outbreak of patriotic songs and thanks to Cousin Usher and wife, the company separated until next year.

—Secretary Pro. Tem.

49TH REESE–GILLETTE REUNION (1919)

The 49th Reese–Gillette reunion was held at the home of Mrs. Esther Bresee on Thursday, August 21, 1919. Fifty-nine cousins were present, coming from Sherburne, Poolville, Norwich, Cortland, Syracuse, Waterville, Deansboro, Brooklyn and Sidney, New York and Cleveland, Ohio. Dinner was served about 1:30 after which remarks were made by several of the cousins and cards from absent ones were read.

Death has removed from our presence during the year

Arthur Chapel and Davis Oliver. The latest birth reported was a daughter to Mr. and Mrs. A. H. Bresee. Leroy Holmes, who has attended every reunion, was prsent as was Mrs. Esther Bresee who has attended 48.

An interesting feature of the program planned and carried out by the president was the introduction of each of the 13 families present and the report from each of the number present and the number absent, showing that there might have been 160 instead of the 59 present. Many of our families were not represented so everyone was requested to make a special effort to have all present next year and have an attendance of 150 or more in honor of the 50th anniversary of the Reese–Gillette Reunions, which will be held at the home of Mr. and Mrs. J. R. Parsons. Officers for next year were appointed as follows: President, Miss Harriet M. Bresee, and Secretary, Miss Una M. Parsons.

—Secretary of the Day

GOLDEN REUNION OF THE REESE–GILLETTE FAMILIES (1920)

The Golden, or 50th, annual Reese–Gillette reunion was held at the home of Mr. and Mrs. John Reese Parsons on Thursday, August 26, 1920. Sixty-four cousins were present, coming from Sherburne, Eaton, Waterville, Norwich, Cincinnatus, Cortland, Elmira, Seneca Falls, and Syracuse, NY; Cleveland, Ohio, Detroit and Niles, Michigan. Thirteen of those cousins were present at the first reunion.

The time before dinner was spent welcoming the cousins, renewing old acquaintances and making new ones. We had with us several who had not been present for many years and others who were present for the first time.

Dinner was served about 1:30 at which time Mrs. Levisa Carrier was presented with a birthday cake, today being her 88th birthday.

As soon as dinner was finished, Harriet Bresee, president, treated the cousins to an interesting program. It consisted of music by Mr. and Mrs. George Nhare and Laura and Walter Chapel; recitations by the Bresee children; history and remarks of our reunions past by Charles Carrier, J. R. Parsons and Dr. F. D. Reese. Letters were read from the absent ones. Telegrams were read from Caroline Oaks Wentworth and Belle Oakes of Cuba and Mr. and Mrs. H. C. Allen, Jr. of Rochester, VT.

In remembrance of the Golden Anniversary, Charles Carrier presented, in behalf of the cousins, gold coins to LeRoy Holmes who has attended every reunion; Mrs. Esther Bresee who has attended 49 reunions and Mrs. Levisa Carrier whose birthday it was and who was the oldest auntie and cousin present.

The officers for next year were appointed as follows: President, Mrs. Howard Eastman; Vice President, Mrs. Ellen Collins Nhare; Secretary, Mrs. Mary Holey.

Since the reunion, word has been received of the death of Mrs. Carrie Reese Fleming at her home in Geneva, NY, on August the 29th.

—Secretary of the Day

THE 52ND REESE–GILLETTE REUNION (1922)

The 52nd annual reunion of the Reese–Gillette families was held at the home of Mr. and Mrs. Gillette Reese just south of this village, on Thursday, August 24, 1922. There were about 40 of the cousins present. After dinner the cousins were called to order by the president of the day, Walter H. Race, and letters were read from those unable to attend this year. Cousin Charles Carrier gave a short talk upon the life of Dr. Frank D. Reese, who was taken away during the year. Miss Clara Bresee recited in a very pleasing manner.

The officers for next year are: President, Miss Una Parsons; Vice President, Russell H. Bresee; Secretary, Mrs. Ola Crandall.

Others who passed from our midst during the year were Mrs. DeForest Lerner of Charleston, Staten Island; Mrs. Lavina Rees Darling of Alpine, Michigan, and Mrs. Reese, mother of Carrie L. Reese of Rome, NY.

Upon the invitation of Mrs. Esther Bresee it was voted to hold the reunion next year at the Bresee home just south of this village. Charles L. Carrier and John R. Parsons were appointed as a committee to adopt resolutions recognizing our cousin Frank D. Reese, which were as follows:

WHEREAS, the All-governing Power has seen in His wise providence to take from our family the highest example of manhood in the person of our dear cousin Dr. F. E. Reese, and

WHEREAS, we as a family in our humble manner wish to express our regret and sorrow to the living, our great loss, it is hereby

RESOLVED, that we, the reunion assembled, have appreciated his example in the world and now mourn his loss and be it further

RESOLVED, that these kindly thoughts be recorded in our family history on this 24th day of August, 1922, and be it further

RESOLVED, that the sympathy of each and everyone present be extended to his widow and little son who sincerely mourn his loss by sending them a copy of these resolutions.

—John L. Parsons, Charles L. Carrier, Committee

A rising note of thanks was extended to Mr. and Mrs. Reese for opening their home for the day, after which the meeting was adjourned.

53RD REESE–GILLETTE REUNION (1923)

The 53rd annual Reese–Gillette reunion was held at the home of Mrs. Esther Bresee on Thursday, August 23, 1923. Cousins were present from Norwich, Stamford, Cortland, Earlville and Rochester, VT. After dinner, which was fully enjoyed by the 40 or so cousins present, letters were read from those who were absent. The following officers were elected for the coming year: President, Miss Elizabeth Reese; Vice President, Miss Clara Bresee; Secretary, Mrs. Ola P. Crandall. Miss Mildred Bresee gave a recitation that was enjoyed by all.

> Cousin LeRoy Holmes is the only cousin who has never missed a reunion. Mrs. Esther Bresee has missed but one and Mrs. Levisa Carrier has missed but few. There was no place named for the next reunion.
>
> —Secretary

THE MICHIGAN REESE REUNIONS (1927 and 1928)

Eugene Reese Huntly and his wife Grace hosted very successful Reese reunions in the summers of 1927 and 1928 at the beautiful old Victorian style home of his grandfather Judson Wade Rees on Barron Lake, Niles, Michigan. Judson was the fourth child of John Melancthon Rees and Angeline Mills, born May 5, 1825. He is listed as Wade J. Rees in the Michigan 1870 Federal Census. The Barron Lake property is listed on the Cass County plat map of 1860, Howard Township, as belonging to J. W. Rees.

Judson Wade Rees married Catherine Marie Willard (1825–1917). They were the parents of two children, Anna Adele born May 21, 1850 and John Judson (1852–1931). John Judson was listed in the Michigan 1870 Federal Census as Judd Rees.

On September 29, 1879 Anna Adele married Gordon Huntly (1850–1908), son of Ephraim and Eliza (Ross) Huntly. Eugene Reese Huntly was the eldest of their four children. Eugene married Grace Elizabeth Doane on June 27, 1906. Anna Adele died on March 30, 1930.

John Marion Rees, born January 31, 1841, the twelfth child of John Melancthon Rees, married Mary Hunter. They had five children, three of whom were school teachers and did not marry. Their second child was named after his grandfather, John Melancthon.

Under John Melancthon's capable leadership there were games and entertainment provided for the children at the reunions. A newspaper account or other record of these reunions was not found. As a boy of twelve, I seem to remember there was a song, short speech or announcements, recognitions, and a blessing asked before eating.

In 1927 two group pictures were taken: one by the house and the other in full sun (Fig. 20.1). The 1927 picture in full sun is too bright to identify faces, however, identifications are made for both the 1927 and 1928 pictures taken by the house (Figs. 20.2—20.5).

FIGURE 20.1
The "sunny" 1927 Reese reunion photo, Niles, MI

FIGURES 20.1 (*top*) and **20.2** (*above*)
1927 Reese reunion photo (Niles) with identifications below

1. Emma Sinclair
2. Charlie Sinclair
3. John M. Reese
4. Frank Reese
5. Nourma Stanley
6. Gladys Johnson
7. Willard Beall
8. Arthur Johnson & Reese

9. Gertrude Johnson
10. Lillian Reese
11. Wesley Andrews
12. Stanley Collins
13. Stella Collins
14. Dagmar Zeiger
15. Wesley Zeiger

16. Alpha Reese
17. Mabel Reese
18. Mary Hunter Reese
19. Dorothy Huntly
20. Harmony Binns
21. Mildren Binns
22. Howard Bower

23. Jacqueline Bower
24. Frank Binns
25. Daniel Zeiger
26. Ruth Johnson
27. Catherine Zeiger
28. Robert Johnson
29. John Johnson

30. Walter Johnson
31. True L. Reese
32. Thelma Zeiger
33. Vernice Zeiger
34. Wesley Zeiger, Jr.
35. Lillian Beall
36. Anna Andrews
37. Ellen Elizabeth Huntly

FIGURES 20.3 (*top*) and **20.4** (*above*)
1928 Reese reunion photo (Niles) with identifications below

1. Anna Andrews
2. Lillian Zeiger
3. Daniel Zeiger
4. True L. Reese
5. Frank Binns
6. Gertrude Johnson
7. Reese Johnson
8. Arthur Johnson
9. Dagmar Zeiger
10. Wesley Zeiger
11. Mona Dunkelberger
12. Catherine Zeiger
13. Robert Johnson
14. Walter Johnson
15. Vernice Zeiger
16. Wesley Zeiger, Jr.
17. John Johnson
18. Ruth Johnson
19. Thelma Zeiger
20. Floyd Dunkelberger
21. Minnie Dunkelberger
22. Wesley Andrews
23. Rev. Stanley Collins
24. Mrs. S. Collins
25. Frank Reese
26. Nourma Stanley
27. Alpha Reese
28. Gladys Johnson
29. Ernest Johnson
30. Harold Beall
31. Maybelle Beall
32. Keith Beall
33. Donald Beall
34. Williard Beall
35. John M. Reese
36. Mildred Binns
37. Elaine Huntly
38. Grace Huntly
39. Eugene R. Huntly
40. Judd Reese
41. Ellen Elizabeth Huntly

Cymru—"Land of Fellow Countrymen"

The identifying icon for the following section, *Part VI—A Rhys Family in Michigan*, is the Welsh emblem Daffodil, whose Welsh word, *cenhinen pedr*, is almost the same as that for leek (cenhinen).

PART VI

A Rhys Family in Michigan

21

THE PIONEER BROTHERS

JACOB Singer Rees was the first of the two brothers to leave the wagon train. He took his family and laid claim to land along a north branch of the St. Joseph River, called Christian Creek. The property, listed in his son's name, in the 1860 plat record, is around 200 acres bordering on the west side of the creek, a short distance south of present-day Adamsville. It is in the south east corner of Ontwa Township.

Jacob and his wife, Anna Mills Rees, brought three daughters, ages 10 to 13, with them. They were named Rebecca, Emmerett, and Nancy. Rebecca married George Lynch in 1838 and bore two children: Norman and Mary. Emmerett married Horace Thompson in 1836 and bore five children: James, Albert

R., Eliza, Nancy S., and George. Nancy married Mahlon B. Gillett in 1839 and bore two boys: Lewis and George. They lived in the east end of Bertrand Township, just south of Niles.

The only son of Jacob and Anna, also named Jacob, was born in Michigan. He married Mertie Miller in 1862 and they became the parents of Blennie and lived on the family farm.

Genevieve Beall Porter, in her *The Reese Family in Michigan,* has suggested that the Jacob S. Rees family settled in Genesee County. The town of Reese, Michigan, east of Saginaw, according to local authorities, was founded by a Mr. G. W. Reese. He was a railroad man with the Huron and Eastern Railway in the late 19th century. A recent news story involving a train noise complaint notes that the Village of Reese owes its name to the railroads. Huron and Eastern is now one of 50 regional railroads owned by RailAmerica, Inc.

Our ancestor, John Melancthon Rees, born May 15, 1796, was the other "pioneer brother" and second son of Jacob and Anna Gillett Rees. The attendance record shows that grandfather, John M., took his wife, Angeline, to the 1873 Rees–Gillett Reunion in New York State when his mother was 100 years of age. Also attending was Mahlon B. and Nancy Rees Gillett from Michigan.

John M.'s unusual middle name came from the name of Martin Luther's close friend, scholar, and professor of Greek, Phillip Melancthon (1497–1560). In 1521 Phillip Melancthon published the first summary of reformation theology. Luther was very enthusiastic with Melancthon's explanation of the doctrines of sin, grace, repentance, and salvation.

John Melancthon and Angeline Rees (Fig. 21.1), coming with eight children, chose 40 acres of land just east of the Cass County line and north of the Indiana state line in Milton Township. At age 19, their first child, Anna Maria (Fig. 21.1), married

John Nyman of Chicago. He was a charter member of the Chicago Board of Trade and owner of a fleet of grain vessels on the Great Lakes known as the *Montgomery Line*.

Angeline lived May 5, 1801 to May 29, 1895. Grace Steeves

FIGURE 21.1
Five Generations of the Nyman Family
(clockwise from lower right) Angeline Mills Rees; daughter, Anna Maria Rees Nyman; great-granddaughter, May Nyman Bliss; grandson, Fay Nyman; great-great-grandson, Lewis Edgar Bliss *(center)*

notes that the baby in Figure 21.1 represents the descendants of the Bliss, Nyman, Cook, Rees, Gillett, Mills, Hollenbeck, Spoor, and Hower families in America.

John M. and Angeline's first son was Jacob, born April 7, 1822. Jacob was 12 years old when he experienced the covered wagon adventure from New York State. He is the subject of the next chapter.

Martha, John and Angeline's second daughter, was born January 19, 1824. She married John C. Collins in 1849 and her family consisted of five children: Albert, Alice, Emma, John, and Effie. Martha was the first historian and charter member of the First Baptist Church of Niles.

Judson Wade was the fourth child of John and Angeline, born May 5, 1825. He married Catherine Marie (Willard) Heath, the widow of Richard Heath, on February 22, 1849. Their daughter, Ann Adelle, was born May 21, 1850 and married Gordon Huntly. Their son, John Judson, died without issue.

Gordon and Ann Adelle Huntly had four children. They were Eugene Reese, Winifred Wade, Mary Louise, and Clarence Gordon.

John and Angeline named their third son Elisha Mills (Fig. 21.2), born November 6, 1827. He married Elizabeth Batchelor and sired four sons. However only Eugene Mills (Figs. 21.2, 21.3), born in 1874, survived to adulthood. The Elisha Mills Rees family owned the Gene Rees Farm (Fig. 22.2), pictured in the next chapter, "The Jacob Rees Family." Elisha died on March 5, 1887. Eugene's son, William (Fig. 21.4), born about 1900, lived in Mishawaka, Indiana.

John and Angeline's third daughter, Sarah, was born September 22, 1829. Sarah married William H. Olmstead on May 6, 1849. Their family consisted of 12 children, three of whom died in a diphtheria epidemic in 1866. The surviving nine

FIGURE 21.2
Elisha Mills and Elizabeth Reese with son, Eugene Mills Rees

Olmstead children were: Eva, who married Moses A. Hulin; Mary Adeline, Mary Elizabeth, Emma Bates, Frank Ernst, Martha Electa, Lillian Maud, William Milton, who married May Brown; and Otis Edward, who married Minnie Kite.

Fourth and fifth daughters were twins, Emmeline and Caroline, born July 11, 1831. Caroline lived only eight months.

FIGURE 21.3
Eugene (Gene) Mills and Ida Rees
50th Anniversary, c. 1945

FIGURE 21.4
William Mills and Vera Ellen Rees,
50th Anniversary, 1967

Emmeline married James L. Fowler. She and James had three sons and a daughter. They were Edwin, Frank, Ida, and Frederick.

The sixth daughter born to the Rees family was Mary Catherine, born July 7, 1833. She was a baby on the covered wagon trip from New York State. She married Cyrus Gillett and lived in the Bertrand Township area, just south of Niles. Mary died on October 7, 1868 at age 35. She had no children.

Esther (Fig. 21.5) was the seventh daughter, born in Michigan on January 7, 1836, one year before Michigan became the 26th state on January 26, 1837. She married William Sinclair on November 26, 1854 and bore six children. Their names were: Ella, William, Charles, Bessie, Otto, and Julia. Esther lived to age 90 and died September 26, 1926.

Eighth daughter, Rebecca Harmony, was born May 20, 1836. She married Castle Chapman on June 25, 1859. She died November 26, 1871 at age 33 (35?). She had no children.

FIGURE 21.5
John Marion Rees and sister, Esther Rees Sinclair, c. 1920

The fourth son of John M. and Angeline was John Marion (Fig. 21.5), born Janaury 31, 1841. John married Mary Hunter in 1868 and six children were born to this union. They were: Alpha, Minnie, John Jr., Frank Hart, Edith Mabel, and Worth. Alpha and John Jr. were dedicated schoolteachers who never married. They were both prominent in the preparation and activities of the Barren Lake Reese reunions of 1927 and 1928. The family lived in Mishawaka, Indiana.

Lewis Cass, the 13th and last child of John M. and Angeline Rees, was born July 5, 1843 and lived only two years.

22
THE JACOB REES FAMILY

J ACOB Rees, the first son of John Melancthon and Angeline Mills Rees, was born in Sherburne, New York on April 7, 1822. He was 12 years of age when he came with the covered wagon train to Michigan, along with his parents, cousins, and Uncle Jacob and Aunt Anna. Two more sisters and a brother were born after the family arrived in Michigan. The family eventually lived in the home on Ironwood Road, north of South Bend, Indiana (Fig. 21.1).

Jacob Rees, my great-grandfather, married Sylvia House in 1851 and later moved to a farm south of Mishawaka, Indiana. A picture of the farm taken more than two generations later and after the turn of the century, has been called The Gene Reese

FIGURE 22.1
THE J. M. Rees home on Ironwood Road

Farm (Fig. 21.2).

Sylvia House, born June 27, 1829 in New York State, was the seventh child in her family of four girls and five boys. The family came to the northern Indiana area and appeared in the 1850 territory census, Porter County. The father, Zela House, was 66 and his wife Eunice Belknap House, born in Vermont, was 65. In the Michigan census, 1850, Berrien County, Sylvia was listed as a housekeeper with the Hambleton family.

FIGURE 22.2
The Lorin Eugene (Gene) Reese Farm home, south of Mishawaka, 1912

It appears the children of Jacob and Sylvia were born at the Indiana location. All of the children are listed in the St. Joseph County, Indiana census of 1870. After the two older sons, James Warren and Judson Wade, left for the west, and father, John Melancthon, died on July 20, 1876, Jacob and Sylvia moved back to the parents' home on Ironwood Road. A third son, Emory Melancthon, died in 1880. Grandmother Angeline lived with Jacob's family until she died on May 29, 1895. The Rees families are buried in the Silverbrook Cemetery, south of Niles.

FIGURE 22.3
Jacob Rees (1822–1893)

Children Judson Wade, True Lincoln, and Angeline Reese are dealt with in subsequent chapters. This is the time when, as the Rees children left home, they added an "e" to their surname. It is not known at this time what happened to Hiram Singer Reese. Among the younger children were the three daughters of Jacob and Sylvia: Angeline, Harmony, and Anna (some places listed as Mary). They were always good friends, enjoying each other's company. They are pictured in Figure 22.4 with their mother.

Harmony, born about 1869, married Frank Binns. They had two daughters, Annabele and Mildred, with married names of Hubrect and Drescher, who lived in the Detroit area.

Anna married Wesley Andrews and lived in Niles, Michigan. They had no children.

FIGURE 22.4
(from left) Sylvia House Rees, Angeline Reese Zeiger,
Harmony Reese Binns, Anna Reese Andrews

After the death of Jacob in 1893, Sylvia moved to the location of her daughter Angeline on the Zeiger farm and lived in the "little house." In 1902 she moved to live with her youngest daughter, Anna, in Niles. She died there on February 23, 1914. Grandmother Sylvia Rees was very highly respected and long remembered by her family and all those who knew her.

23
THE REES HOME CHURCH

THE FIRST Baptist Church of Niles, Michigan is not only the most historic church in the area, but was also the church home of our ancestor, John Melancthon Rees. About 1834 John came here with his wife and eight children—ages 10 and under—as a pioneer family. They settled near the southwest corner of Milton Township. The seeds of the church were planted in the Carey Mission as noted in the historical accounts in the *History of Berrien and Van Buren Counties, 1800.*

Isaac McCoy was called by the American Baptist Missionary

Society to seek out a likely place for a mission school in the wilderness of the St. Joseph River Valley. On October 9, 1822 he established a mission to the Pottawatomie Indians on a U.S. Government land grant of one square mile, just one mile west of the present Broadway Bridge in Niles. It was named the Carey Mission in honor of the great Baptist missionary, William Carey. A Michigan Historical Marker indicates the location.

Reverend McCoy, with a Mr. Jackson, four hired men and some Indian boys from his Ft. Wayne School, arrived at the site to set up the mission. They came with two oxen drawn wagons, one four-horse wagon and four cows. Rev. McCoy returned to Ft. Wayne within the month for his wife Christina and family of five children. Returning, he brought six laboring men and eighteen pupils. Some rode in the wagons; however, many walked the long cold miles or rode horse-back. The 95-mile trip took ten days. Upon returning on December 18, he found a shortage of flour and vital supplies. It was noted "as God supplied manna in the desert," so our Heavenly Father provided food to sustain His children in the wilderness of St. Joseph Valley. New supplies arrived in February.

A large Indian village stood close to the Carey Mission. A few white settlers who lived nearby joined their Indian brethren to worship Christ at the mission. As news of the Carey Mission spread east, more pioneer settlers began to follow. They were attracted by the influence of the mission and access to the river, which provided transportation, power for a mill and trade opportunities with the Indians. The mission flourished and became the headquarters for the Indians and the white settlers. They worshipped and traded peacefully together. The purpose of the Carey Mission was two-fold: to convert the Indians and to encourage settlement of the fertile land.

Chapter 23—The Rees Home Church

The Carey Mission was closed in late 1832 after the government started to move the Indians west. The Indians, by persuasion and force, started down the old Sauk Trail. With a heavy heart, Isaac McCoy joined his Indian brethren on their long sorrowful march. His last words were, "Tell the brethren to never let the Indian mission decline."

On August 5, 1841 sixteen community people claiming membership in regular Baptist churches met in a schoolhouse with the intention of forming a First Baptist Church. One of these charter members was John Johnson, who arrived in the area in 1825. He lived and worked as a blacksmith and shoemaker at the mission. He was the first white settler in what was to become Berrien Township. Another member, Baldwin Jenkins, a judge under the old territorial law, arrived with his family in 1824.

A third charter member was John Melancthon Rees who happened to be the first person to sign on and also the first person to receive the right hand of fellowship as the Advisory Council of Churches, meeting August 14, 1841, approved The Articles of Faith and Covenant. Charter member S. S. Lewis acted as moderator for the founding meetings and J. P. Martin acted as clerk. The Advisory Council consisted of nine members from the Baptist churches of Pleasant Lake, Kingsbury, Rolling Prairie and Centerville.

The charter membership of nine men and seven women also included Joseph Howell, William Cotton, Lewis Fellows and William Mead, Jr. The women signers were Susanna Carbury, Sally Bailey, Sally Bennett, Lucy Fellows, Lucy Thompson, Christina Howell and Clarissa Nicholson. An extra meeting was called for on December 6, 1841 to receive by letter, Martha Rees, daughter of John Rees, who was appointed church historian.

The first church was a small white frame building with a square belfry. The cornerstone was laid June 1, 1844. The First Baptist Church of the village of Niles was occupied January 1, 1845.

Discipline in the church was strict. Although travel may have been difficult at times, the leaders as well as the people were charged for failure to attend services. It was a time of absolutes. Nevertheless, membership grew rapidly as the village grew. By 1877 plans were made for a new building. The new building was built on the same site at which is now Fourth and Broadway. The structure was a large white frame New England style building with a high steeple (Fig. 23.1).

FIGURE 23.1
First Baptist Church, Niles

The first service was held November 9, 1878. It was noted in the newspaper that, "the heart of every church member responded to the spirit of the inscription on the threshold of their new house of worship." The plaque reads, "Enter into His gates with thanksgiving and into His courts with praise" (Psalm 100:4).

This was the church home of the Rees families for many generations. The related families of Gillette, Huntly, Andrews, and Willard were also prominent in the church.

A review of early church records revealed a number of names

of the Rees family and those who may be related to them. It all started with J. M. (John) Rees, a charter member. Most family members now write the name ending with an "e" (Reese). Some names taken from the membership rolls as they were added over a period of years, are as follows:

    12/06/1841 — Martha Rees, by letter
    01/14/1848 — Jacob Rees, by letter
    11/05/1844 — I. H. Gillett, by letter
    11/05/1844 — Mabel Gillett, by letter
    12/29/1849 — Mahlon Gillett, by letter
    12/29/1849 — Charles Gillett, by letter
    01/11/1850 — Emeline Reese, by letter
    04/06/1850 — Nancy Gillett, by baptism
    06/08/1850 — Mary Gillett, by letter
    04/19/1851 — Wade Reese, by letter
    02/17/1855 — Sylvia Rees, by baptism
    02/03/1855 — Mary (Anna) Rees, by baptism
    03/06/1855 — Harmony Rees, by baptism
    04/25/1866 — Anna Huntly, by baptism
    07/30/1893 — Mary Huntly, by baptism
    09/14/1904 — Mary (Anna) Andrews, by letter
    10/30/1904 — Wesley Andrews
    02/06/1910 — Nellie Huntly, by letter from Cassopolis
    04/1921 — Mr. and Mrs. Judson Rees
    1922 — Ellen Reese
    12/02/1928 — George Willard, by baptism
    04/26/1931 — Ruth Willard, by baptism

CENTENNIAL

The church celebrated its centennial in 1941 with a pageant that involved the narration and portrayal of historical events in the life of the church. A Centennial Hymn was written by Mrs. Roselyn Steere and sung to the tune of *The Battle Hymn of the Republic.*

On the 125th anniversary of First Baptist Church, February 6, 1966, the congregation held their first service in a new edifice at 15th and Main Street in Niles. The historic cornerstone was moved to the new church and the old church on Broadway was demolished.

A little over a century after First Baptist Church was founded, a second Baptist church was founded within the heritage of the Rees family. According to the *Tri-County Atlas,* first published in 1860, "J. W. Rees owned 240 acres of property, less about 50 acres, that are a part of the southwest end of Barron Lake." Judson Wade Rees was born May 5, 1825 in Sherburne, New York and at an early age came to Michigan with his parents, John M. and Angeline (Mills) Rees. Judson Wade, usually called Wade, married Catherine Marie Willard, also born in New York State on June 16, 1825.

There were two children from this marriage: Ann Adelle and Judd. Judd married Ellen Green. There were no children from this marriage. Ann Adelle married Gordon Huntly on September 29, 1879. They had four children: Eugene R., Winfred W., Louise, and Clarence G.

Eugene Reese Huntly (1880–1954) inherited a large part, if not all, of his grandfather's property on Barron Lake. The Huntly Memorial Baptist Church was built on this property south of Reese Drive. Mr. Huntly died only days after donating the land for the new church. Friends of the Huntlys, Mr. and Mrs. Ed Dreher, bought an adjacent plot of ground to add to the space.

In the early 1950's Rev. Ray L. McCoy, serving as pastor of First Baptist Church, purchased an old school bus and began

FIGURE 23.2
Huntly Memorial Baptist Church, Niles

picking up children and some parents in the Barron Lake area for services in the Niles church. It soon became his dream to see a church built for the people in the growing Barron Lake area. After a survey of families by State Convention officers showed a definite interest, the church was organized and met in a school until a building could be constructed.

On May 5, 1955 thirty-four members of First Baptist Church, Niles were dismissed to become charter members of the new church, Huntly Memorial Baptist. Men of both churches and interested men of the community with building talents constructed the simple building (Fig. 23.2). Rev. McCoy pastored both churches until May 1956 when Rev. Norman A. Sundwall became the first full-time pastor. Average attendance had increased to 144 by the time Rev. Sundwall resigned June 15, 1960.

A parsonage and two additions to the church have been constructed, including more Sunday School rooms, baptistry, foyer, and space for social occasions. The church, although relatively small, is very friendly and serves the community well. As of 2002 the membership was 93 with 25 additional regular attendees. In October 1967 Huntly Memorial Baptist Church was recognized as "Church of the Year" in the "Under 200 Members" category by the State Baptist Convention.

This brief history of Huntly Memorial Baptist Church was taken from data on the Huntly, Reese, and Willard families.

24

THE JUDSON WADE REESE FAMILY

JUDSON Wade Reese, born August 21, 1854 and named after his uncle, was born in St. Joseph County, Indiana. He was listed as "Wade" in the Indiana 1870 Census. Judson was the second son of Jacob and Sylvia House Rees, who were the parents of eight children—five sons and three daughters. This was a young family before, during, and after the Great Civil War.

It seemed that the local farming community had little to offer a young man in the years just after the Civil War. Many men and boys over a certain age had their own riding horse and were enthused at the thought of going west.

Jesse James (1847–1882) rode with William Quanticill's raids during the Civil War and attacked Lawrence, Kansas in 1863, burning the town and murdering 150 civilians. By 1870 however, it was commonly known that the pioneer trails west, including the Santa Fe and Chisholm trails, were safe and becoming popular thoroughfares for covered wagons as well as the would-be cowboy looking for a new life.

In the absence of definitive evidence, it can be assumed that Judson Wade and James Warren Reese received the blessing of their pioneer grandfather, John Melancthon Rees, and left their Indiana home together around 1875. The third brother, Emory M., was not so inclined. He may not have had the stamina of his brothers who were two and three years older, respectively. Emory died at about 25 years of age of causes not on record.

John Melancthon Rees, a loving grandfather to many, died July 26, 1876. Grandmother Angeline Mills Rees, living to age 95, died May 29, 1895. They were our original pioneers.

The brothers, Judson Wade and James Warren, may have stayed together as far as central Kansas where good land was still available to those agreeing to occupy and cultivate it. It is also thought that Judson met his wife-to-be on the trail west. He married Mary Jane Crakes, born October 21, 1856. According to their youngest daughter Alpha, they arrived in a covered wagon and lived near the Yaggy Plantation. They raised a family of twelve—five boys and seven girls.

James, who went by his middle name, Warren, may have had other thoughts. He was likely still single and, as we are told, traveled on to Oregon. There may be some descendants in Oregon. Judson, it appears, kept in contact with his Michigan cousins and is known to have visited them on one occasion.

Chapter 24—The Judson Wade Reese Family   235

FIGURE 24.1
Four Reese Brothers
(from left) Cephas Crakes ("C. C." born October 30, 1891); Otto Frank (born April 16, 1889); Wade Harlow (born November 30, 1886); and Thomas Jacob (born December 4, 1884)

Four of the five Judson Wade Reese boys grew to manhood in central Kansas. They made an impressive picture as shown in Figure 24.1, taken in about 1910.

A younger brother, George Dewey, was born April 27, 1896 and apparently was named after Admiral George Dewey who became famous at the time of the Spanish-American War, before the turn of the century. George lived less than eight years, dying March 6, 1904.

The seven daughters all grew to womanhood and married. The first to pass away was Myrtle, born August 26, 1881 and living to age 39. She was married to George Bowser (Fig. 24.3) and they were the parents of a daughter, Vida, born October 4, 1905 in Reno County, Kansas. Vida married William Davis, Jr. Sometime after the death of Myrtle in 1920, a family picture

FIGURE 24.2
The Judson Wade Reese Family, Hutchinson, Kansas—1920
(back) Mary, Grace, Farie, Sylvia, and Wade
(middle) C. C., Otto, Alpha, Blanche, and Tom
(front) Grandpa Judson Wade Reese and Grandma Mary Jane Reese

FIGURE 24.3
George and Myrtle Reese Bowser

was taken on the steps of the family home (Fig. 24.2). Vida died on October 3, 1976 in Hutchinson, Kansas.

This was a close family, mourning the loss of their sister and daughter, shown in her wedding picture, around 1900 (Fig. 24.3).

A summary of the other Judson Wade Reese families from the early twentieth century follows. Additional narrative is given as available.

The eldest daughter was Blanche Annis Reese (Fig. 24.2) (born November 24, 1876; died May 1969) who married Minor C. Arnold. They had two children: Milburn Cephas, born December 12, 1900 and Inez, born July 28, 1903.

Milburn Cephas Arnold married Jennie Marie Johnson (born July 17, 1909) of Astmark, Sweden in Hooker, Oklahoma. Milburn and Jennie had five children. James Minor (born December 19, 1927; died May 1993) married Darlene Blankenship. They had three children. Esther Leone (born January 7, 1931; died August 1988) married Robert C. Finfrock. They had four children. Thomas Duane (born July 29, 1940; died July 14, 1975), married Tina Dale Loper, who also died July 14, 1975. Mildred Ann, born April 24, 1943, married Kelley Davis. Mary Jane, born January 25, 1946, married but had no children.

Inez Mary Arnold (born July 28, 1903; died April 16, 1958 in Delta County, Colorado) married Tom Henry Hurd. They were the parents of two children. Eva Lee was born October 29, 1919 and married James E. Clark. Emory Mills was born December 14, 1921 and

FIGURE 24.4
Blanche A. Reese Arnold and son, Milburn Arnold, 1925, when Milburn was leaving home for the California oil fields. It was there that he met Jennie Johnson.

FIGURE 24.5
Julius E. Patterson and Grace Alice Reese Patterson of Hutchinson, Kansas

married Lois M. Splittstoesser. They were the parents of two children. Emory died September 4, 1991.

Inez and her second husband, Winfield Tuttle, were the parents of Helen Marie Tuttle, born June 15, 1931.

The second daughter in the Judson Wade Reese family was Grace Alice (born January 4, 1879; died April 1, 1955 in Sweetwater, Texas). Grace married Julius Patterson (1879–1951). They (Fig. 24.5) had two sons: Arleigh (1900–1964) who married Ruth Allen, and Julius Wesley (1907–1972) who married Maribel Bland.

The third child was daughter Myrtle, of whom we have already written.

The fourth daughter in the family was Mary (1883–1932). She was married to Robert Arthur. Mary (Fig. 24.2) died in an automobile accident and is buried in Forrest Lawn Cemetery near Hollywood, CA.

The first son in the family was Thomas Jacob, as noted in the photo of the Reese boys on page 235. Tom married Lena Etta Schrayer (1915–1997). Their children were Sylvia Genelle, born 1936; Thomas Judson, born 1938; and Harold Keith.

The second son was Wade Harlow, noted in the boys' photo. He married Margaret "Maggie" Hobson. They had no children.

The third son was Otto (p. 235), who married Alice Theiss.

Their children were Dorothy (1928–1987), Charles Cephas, born in 1930, and Willis Edward.

The fourth son was Cephas Crakes (p. 235). In March 2004 Joyce D. Reese summarized her father-in-law's life as follows.

FIGURE 24.6
C. C. and Melba Reese, 1952

"Cephas was born in Reno County, Kansas on October 30, 1891. He was known as 'C. C.' and was raised on a farm near Hutchinson, Kansas. He was the eighth of 12 children. As a young man he moved to Cheyenne Wells, Colorado where he met and married Melba Fern Akerly whose father was the Manual Training teacher at the local high school. C. C. and Melba (Fig. 24.6) lived there for a short time before moving to Greeley, Colorado where he worked in an auto repair shop. Their first two children were born in Greeley and the last two in Cheyenne Wells. In 1927 he moved his family to Lamar, Colorado and opened the Reese Motor Company (Fig. 24.7). It remained in business for 66 years.

"C. C. and Melba had four children. The first was Helen Louise (born May 26, 1918; died April 30, 1984) who was married to Milton James Proett. They were the parents of two daughters: Nancy Jean, born in 1941 and Connie Christine, born in 1946.

"C. C. and Melba's second daughter was Myrtle Leone (1920–1998) who was married to Robert Senier. They were the parents of Sally Jo, born in 1950.

"C. C. and Melba were also the parents of two boys: James

FIGURE 24.7
Reese Motor Company, Lamar, Colorado

Allan, who died at age 19, and Warren Eugene. Warren followed in his father's footsteps, leading an active life in the business community. He operated the Reese Motor Company for 40 years.

"C. C. was active in community affairs in Lamar and was a member of the Rotary Club, active in Red Cross work, served as Prowers County chairman for two years and on the City Council from 1935 through 1946. He was mayor protem from 1942–1946. C. C. was a member of the First Methodist Church and served on the church's Board of Trustees. He was also a member and past patron of Lamar Chapter No. 112 O.E.S. He was a member of Cheyenne Wells Masonic Lodge No. 132, AF & AM, and served as worshipful master in 1922. He was also a member of the Royal Arch Chapter No. 32, Oriental Council No. 15, and Southern Colorado Consistory at Pueblo.

"C. C. Reese passed away July 3, 1954 in Lamar, Colorado, just prior to his 63rd birthday, and was buried in Fairmont

Cemetery, Prowers County, Colorado."

Warren Reese's life has also been summarized by his wife, Joyce, in the following paragraphs.

"Warren Eugene Reese was born November 24, 1923 in Cheyenne Wells, Colorado to C. C. and Melba F. Reese. He moved to Lamar with his family around the age of three. Warren was the third of four children. He attended Lamar public schools, graduating in 1942. He attended the School of Engineering at Colorado State University in Fort Collins.

"On December 15, 1942 Warren enlisted in the army at Fort Collins and served 30 months in the European Theater of Operations. He was honorably discharged on April 21, 1946 at

FIGURE 24.8
The Warren E. Reese Family
(from left) Jim, Suzanne, Joyce, Cheryl, Warren, and "Sandy"

Fort Leavenworth, Kansas. He returned to Lamar and attended Lamar Community College while at the same time pursuing a career as a partner in his father's new car business. This partnership soon became an agency for Chrysler/Plymouth/Dodge.

"Warren was united in marriage to Joyce Dianne McKitrick in June of 1956 in Wiley, Colorado, and to this union were born three children. Cheryl Kay was born August 28, 1957 and married Donald Novey. James Cullen was born August 30, 1959 and died January 8, 1997. Suzanne Lynn was born April 11, 1963.

"Warren was also in a partnership with the Honda motorcycle dealership from 1972 to 1978. He ran a farm equipment tractor agency from 1975 to 1982 as well as an oil and petroleum jobbership from 1950 to 1982.

"Warren was active as a real estate appraiser and an auctioneer from 1973–1993. He was also active in civic matters including past president and director of the Lamar Chamber of Commerce (1955–1956), area director of the Colorado Automobile Dealers Association for 20 years, Lamar Community Building Director, past president of Lamar Kiwanis Club, past Chairman of the Board of the United Methodist Church, past Worthy Mason of Lamar Masonic Lodge, and a member of Alkay Shriners of Pueblo. A United States Army World War II veteran, he was elected to the Lamar City Charter Committee and was a member of the Lamar Rotary Club.

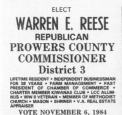

"Warren passed away on January 18, 1993 in Lamar, Colorado at age 69, just four days after his mother, Melba, had died."

The fifth daughter in the Judson Wade Reese family was Farie Pearl, born January 2, 1893. She married Ivan Groff and their children were Gene, who fathered two sons, and Iva, who married Charles Hotchkiss. They lived in Denver and had no children.

The sixth daughter was Sylvia Gertrude, born March 17, 1895. She married Charles S. Counts and their children were Kenneth Wesley, born December 3, 1917; Charles Lowell, born November 13, 1919; Robert Wade, born August 25, 1922; and Hiram R. "Jack," born February 20, 1925.

All four boys served in the military during World War II.

Kenneth Wesley married Lois Evelyn Johnson. He served in the Army.

Charles Lowell married Floriene Messina and served in the Navy from 1943 to 1945 aboard the *USS Natoma Bay*. He was in 13 major battles. Charles and Floriene became the parents of Judith Kay, born in 1943, and Sherry Lynn, born in 1946.

Robert Wade married Dorothy Paglasotta and served in the Navy. Their children were Jerry and Donna. Robert died November 23, 2000.

Hiram Reese ("Jack") was married more than once. He was in the Navy and later in the Army and received a Purple Heart. His children are listed as Charles Joseph, Jack Walter, Penny Kay, and Christopher Duane.

The seventh daughter and twelfth child in the Judson Wade Reese family was Alpha, born May 2, 1900. She married Francis (Frank) R. Blew (1896–1973) on June 9, 1918. They had five children—two girls and three boys.

As a young man, Frank owned a threshing machine with his brother and did custom work with it for several years before he married Alpha. Frank became a major wheat farmer around the Castleton area, which is about 10 miles south of Hutchinson, Kansas. In the late 1930's he bought 500 acres of land in Kingman County, about 30 miles south of Hutchinson. There Frank and his brother "built" a herd of white-faced Hereford cattle. In the late 1950's the land in Kingman County was sold and some 1,300 acres purchased on the McPherson-Rice County line, which is Plum Street north out of Hutchinson.

Melba Maxine, the oldest child of Alpha and Frank was born in 1920. She married Kenneth G. Hutton (1917–1991). She and Kenneth ran a grocery store in Mt. Hope, Kansas for several years before moving to Shell Knob, Missouri. There they ran a resort for a number of years before retiring. They became the parents of Melba Kathlene, born April 26, 1945, and Glen Steven. Kathlene married a man named Ray and they had one daughter, Ashley Kathleen. She is a teacher and has taught piano lessons to many students. Glen, also known as Steve, was born February 24, 1947, married Cheri Lynn Williams, and had three daughters: Katie, Lindsey, and Courtney. They lived in Shell Knob for many years.

A son, Francis Lee "Frankie, Jr." (born February 17, 1926; died March 13, 2004), lived one and a half miles west of Castleton except for time serving in the U.S. Navy during World War II. He married LoRee Reid on February 15, 1947. They had five children: Sharon Lea, Diana Marie, Rex Alan, Gerald "Jerry" Lee, and Karen Kay.

Frankie, Jr. served on various boards in Castleton Township for ten years. He served on the Ambulance and Fire Board for several years as well as on several committees. He was a farmer/stockman and retired after having double bypass heart surgery in August of 1988. He died in his sleep of heart failure in 2004.

Sharon, born in 1947, married Robert Kent Brown and had

FIGURE 24.9
The Francis L. "Frankie, Jr." Blew Family
(back) Frankie, Jr.; Jerry; and Rex Alan
(front) LoRee, Karen, Sharon, and Diana

three sons: Christopher Kent in 1967, Robert Scott in 1970, and Michael Anthony in 1973.

Diana Marie, born in 1949, married Jack Wilbur Kranze and had three children: Jason Robert in 1976, Alicia Marie in 1978, and Jennifer Marie in 1982.

Rex Alan, born in 1955, married Jody Ann Rose and had three sons: Clinton Jay in 1977, Russell Ryan in 1979, and Darren Avery in 1981.

Gerald "Jerry" Lee, born in 1962, married Mary Elizabeth Koehler in 1985 and they had two sons: Justin Wade in 1986 and Lucas Allan in 1991.

Karen Kay, born in 1966, married Dean Duane Johnson at Castleton, Kansas on February 12, 2000 and has one son, Jesse Lee, born June 29, 2001.

The second son of Alpha and Frank, Sr. was Robert Rex, born July 5, 1934 in Hutchinson, Kansas. He married Carol Jane Sutton on March 22, 1957. They had three sons: Robert Larry (born January 30, 1958; died July 2004); Danny Wade, born April 15, 1960 in Sterling, Colorado; and Paul Vincent, born April 11, 1962. Robert lived most of his adult life in Sterling and Haver, Montana.

The third son was Ross Reese, born January 4, 1936 in Hutchinson, Kansas. He married Kathaleen Peterson in 1955 and they became the parents of three children: Curtis Ray in 1955, Pamela Kay in 1958, and Kenneth Wayne in 1960.

The fifth child of Alpha and Frank, Sr. was Carol Eleanor, called "Carolee," born May 5, 1942. She married Dale Reschke in 1961 and they had two children: Alan Wayne (1962–1984) and Sherri Nanette in 1964. Carolee was killed in an auto accident on December 31, 1964 and is buried in Little River, Kansas.

Frank, Sr. and Alpha Reese Blew belonged to Faith Baptist Church of Hutchinson. Frank suffered a stroke in 1972 and died on October 12, 1973. Alpha passed away on September 14, 1977. On September 17, the day Alpha was buried, an article and picture (Fig. 24.10) appeared in the Hutchison newspaper. The story essentially went as follows.

> . . . Mrs. Alpha Reese Blew rummaged through her scrapbook and came up with this photograph of her two sisters, Blanche Arnold of Rago and Myrtle Bowser of Darlow as they enjoyed the 1906 Fair and Agricultural Exhibits.
>
> Mrs. Blew had six sisters and five brothers. The only survivors of the family are her and her sister, Mrs. Sylvia Counts of Denver. Her parents were the late Judson W. Reese and his wife, Jane, who came to

Hutchinson in a covered wagon and lived near the Yaggy Plantation, and later, west of Darlow.

Mrs. Blew now lives at Blue Top Hereford Ranch, north of Inman.

POSTCARD from the 1906 Fair shows considerably different styles, but little difference in the emphasis of the Fairs of today — agriculture.

FIGURE 24.10
Newspaper clipping showing Alpha Reese Blew's sisters, Myrtle Reese Bowser *(left)* and Blanche Reese Arnold at the 1906 Fair, later designated the Kansas State Fair

25

THE TRUE LINCOLN REESE FAMILY

TRUE Lincoln Reese was born at home in St. Joseph County, Indiana on September 5, 1860 to Jacob and Sylvia House Rees. He was the fourth boy in the family of eight children: five boys and three girls. They later moved to the Milton Township, Michigan home (Fig. 22.1, p. 222) near the north end and east side of present day Ironwood Road. A large house has recently replaced it. True grew up at this rural location where it appears the family raised chickens and garden crops. Jacob owned the land on both sides of Ironwood Road, as far south as State Line

Road on the Indiana-Michigan border.

The newly formed Republican Party nominated Abraham Lincoln for President of the United States within days of the birth of True Reese. Lincoln was greatly admired by the Rees family as a man of a very humble background, but endowed with a penetrating intellect. Likewise "Uncle" True grew to manhood as an honest, humble man with deep convictions and understanding.

It is understood that the Sherrill family, relatives of the Drew family and the Rees family, lived near each other in the area southeast of Niles. They attended the Baptist Church in Niles. The children of Jacob and Sylvia added an "e" to the Rees surname.

True's sister, Angeline, and her husband, Daniel Zeiger, were planning to buy the Charles Sherrill farm in Chikaming Township, north of Three Oaks. True Reese and May Sherrill, the daughter of Charles and Hannah Sherrill, planned to be married in the First Baptist Church of Niles. The wedding was performed on August 15, 1888 by the Reverend Charles Ager. This was the home church of the Rees family, where John Melancthon Rees, True's grandfather, was the first to receive the right hand of fellowship and membership in the new church on August 14, 1841. Kate Sherrill, May's elder sister, owned the 40-acre farm across the road to the west of her parent's place. Kate, expecting to move with her parents to Niles, had agreed to sell her farm to May and her new husband. Following the wedding, Charles and Hannah Sherrill, the two couples, and the three Zeiger children went to the Berrien County courthouse in Berrien Springs to file wedding papers as well as complete the sale of the farm to Daniel and Angeline Zeiger. True and May Reese purchased Kate Sherrill's farm some months later, on April 6, 1889, for $2000 (17).

The children of True and May Sherrill Reese, in order of birth were: Rex, Max, Ruth, Robert, Charles, and Harold. It was in this rural community that many of the five Reese children and the seven Zeiger children played, went to school, and grew up together. The relationship was good. Four names of the Reese children were remembered and used in the next generation for the Zeiger grandchildren. They are Rex, Robert, Ruth and Harold.

The True Reese family moved in April of 1902 to a small farm near West Olive, Michigan, a rural community near the Pigeon River, between Holland and Grand Haven. True's sister Harmony, with her husband, Frank Binns, and their two daughters, Mildred and Annabelle, lived in the West Olive community and influenced her brother to move to the area. Five children were born prior to the move. Harold, the youngest, was born in West Olive on December 8, 1904. Their home in West Olive was a two-story log house as shown in the picture (Fig. 25.1) taken in the summer of 1902.

The photo was taken by a local photographer with the intent to sell copies to True on postal cards. Rex sent this card to his cousin, Gertrude, on December 29, 1902, saying, "Happy New Year."

Rex Sherrill Reese, the eldest son of True and May Reese, was born on the farm north of Three Oaks on May 24, 1889. He was 13 when the family moved to West Olive. On September 20, 1910 he married Grace S. Sankey of West Olive, Michigan. Grace, born January 30, 1890, was the daughter of Eli and Fanni VanderMalen Sankey.

There were six children born to Rex and Grace. The family lived in Wayne, Michigan. The children, born between 1912 and 1924, were Helen Ruth, Royal Sankey, Shirley Mae, Stanley Harold, Raymond William, and Stanten Lloyd. At age four, Stanley, born April 21, 1918, ran out into the street to meet his father and was run over by a car and killed. He was, no doubt, an

FIGURE 25.1
Log home of True L. Reese family in West Olive, Michigan *(from left)* children Charles; Robert; Ruth (who was visiting at the time); Grandmother Sylvia Rees, 73 (seated, also visiting); May; True; Max; and Rex

early victim of a common occurrence in the years to come causing the deaths of many small children.

Max Jacob Reese, the second son born to True and May Reese, was born on November 4, 1890 while his parents lived on the farm near Three Oaks, Michigan. He attended the Drew School with his Zeiger cousins: Gertrude, a year older, and Roy, a year younger. At age 11 Max, with his parents, sister, and brothers, moved to West Olive, Michigan. Following high school and military service during World War I, Max attended Hope College in Holland, Michigan where he obtained a Bachelor of Arts degree. Max presumably served with the Michigan

National Guard where he was a 2nd Lieutenant in the Field Artillery and trained at Camp Grayling, Michigan.

At Hope College Max met his wife-to-be, Florence Vyn. They were married in June of 1920 in Grand Haven, Michigan following her graduation from Hope. Max found employment with the Fuller Brush Company in Lima, Ohio. It was at this location their first child, Thomas Vyn, was born, on April 29, 1924. Soon thereafter they moved to Indianapolis, Indiana where Max spent the next 25 years as a Branch Manger for the company. A second child, Virginia Maxine, was born on May 22, 1926.

During his lifetime, Max was a Ruling Elder in four Presbyterian churches, covering a 40-year period. At about 60 years of age he retired from the Fuller Brush Company, moved to Bakersfield, California and served as a real estate broker. He died on November 20, 1972 at age 82.

Thomas Vyn Reese, the son of Max and Florence, obtained his degree as Doctor of Medicine from the Indiana University in 1946. After graduation he joined the United States Air Force as a flight surgeon with the rank of Captain. He served from 1947 into 1949. Thomas married Patricia Ora in 1946 and the first of their three children, Thomas Vyn Jr., was born on April 12, 1947.

Thomas moved to California following his military service and in his life as a doctor, served in many organizations including hospitals, medical societies, foundations, etc. He was chosen "Outstanding Young Man of the Year—1955" in Bakersfield, California (60).

Ruth, the only daughter of True and May Sherrill Reese, was born December 6, 1891 while her parents still lived on the farm in Chikaming Township, Three Oaks, Michigan. At the age of three, Ruth was given in custody to her mother's sister, Kate (Mrs. D. I. Boardman), to rear. The Boardmans lived in

Buchanan and had no children. The Reese family was raising five boys (four at that time) with very modest means. Ruth visited her family for a month each year after they moved to West Olive. She would also visit the Zeiger cousins, her grandmother, Sylvia Rees, and Aunt Anna Andrews.

Ruth graduated from the Buchanan schools, studied piano in Niles, and attended Monticello College in Illinois. In December 1912 she married Dee Earl Ellsworth with whom she bore a son, Sherrill Ellsworth, on October 8, 1913. Sherrill enlisted in the Marines and served in the Pacific Theatre during World War II. He later attended Occidental College, The Chicago Academy of Fine Arts and studied painting under Vaughn Shoemaker, a Nobel Prize winner. Sherrill died in September 1968, just before his 55th birthday.

Ruth was always pleased with her care and the opportunities she had as a child. In her adult life, on the other hand, she experienced troubling times with the early deaths of her first and second husbands. O. Gaylord Marsh, her second husband, was an international lawyer serving in the United States Foreign Service in China and Korea when both nations were unstable prior to World War II. Ruth's "first love" was art. She often spoke of the beauty of Peking, China. When her husband was assigned to Seoul, she completed some 50 oil paintings of "Old Korea," then occupied by the Japanese.

Ruth's third husband, Mirto E. Bigsby, was from an Upper Michigan family of Scottish descent. He built a sizable moving business in Niles, which he left to his two sons. Prior to his death in 1968, he and Ruth moved to Salinas, California, four years before her brother, Max, died. Ruth died there in 1982. (60)

Robert Orville Reese was born June 26, 1893, the fourth child of True and May Reese in Chikaming Township, Berrien

County, Michigan. The farming family moved to West Olive when Robert was nine years old. Sixteen years later, in 1918, he married a neighbor girl, Maggie Maud Hugger. After serving in the Signal Corps during World War II, he tried his hand at sales for the Fuller Brush Company in Detroit. By 1920 he was back farming in Williamston, Michigan. It was here that his three children were born: Thea Mae in 1920, Florence Maxine in 1922, and Robert Orville, Jr. in 1923.

The family purchased an 80-acre dairy farm on Aurelius Road in Mason, Michigan where they also produced sugar beets and field corn. In 1944 they purchased and moved to a 180-acre farm on Wood Road in Lansing, Michigan. It was here that Robert, Sr. and Robert, Jr. farmed together and Robert Sr.'s(?) wife, Maggie, started a project of selling sweet corn, which became a much-anticipated event each summer in the Lansing area. Still today, the opening of the Reese Farm Market is synonymous with summer.

In 1964 Robert, Sr. and Maggie built a new home on an additional 40 acres they had purchased in 1955. They resided there until their deaths. The farm is operated today by their grandson, Robert Orville III. Robert, Jr. died in 1972.

Robert, Sr. and Maggie were founding members of Inter City Bible Church and were both faithful members, serving in many different capacities. Upon retiring in the 1970's they began wintering at their home in St. Petersburg, Florida, until Robert's death in 1987 at age 93. Maggie died in 1997, two months short of her 101st birthday.

Thea Mae married Kenneth Kurtz and they raised a family of seven which included two sets of twins.

Maxine married Clifford Cooley. They had five children including one set of twins.

Robert, Jr. married June Root and had four children. It is their son, Robert Orville, III who continues to farm the Reese Farm in the Lansing, Michigan area as of the summer of 2005.

(The Robert O. Reese family information was contributed by Shirley Hoover and Maxine Cooley.)

Charles Herbert was the fourth son of True Lincoln and May Sherrill Reese, born October 23, 1894, at their Chickaming Township farm. He did not have the privilege of completing high school. After completing the 8th grade, he was needed at home to help on the farm. This was a disappointment to his mother as she had hopes of Charles becoming a doctor. He was very close to his mother and her early death was a great grief to him. He became a rural mail carrier and served in World War I. After the war he attended Ferris Institute in Mt. Pleasant, Michigan and attended Bliss Electrical School in Washington D.C., financing his schooling by working as a Fuller Brush salesman.

Following his schooling and electrical apprenticeship, he worked wiring homes and small businesses.

Charles met Gladys Larrabee at a series of evangelistic meetings held at the Methodist Church in Williamston, Michigan. After a year of courtship, mostly by mail, they were married June 6, 1925. They lived a short time in Wyandotte, Michigan where their first child, Charles Warren, was born on March 13, 1926. He suffered a birth injury to the cervical spine that left him with a seizure disorder. He died June 15, 1935 at age nine. In seeking medical help for Warren, Charles and Gladys were often misunderstood and rebuffed because doctors knew so little about seizure disorders at that time.

Their second son, Albert Denton, was born September 7, 1927, after their move to Williamston, Michigan. He died at the early age of 41, on June 27, 1969, of a massive heart attack. He had three children: Mary Katherine, born November 21, 1955; Richard Larrabee, born August 27, 1963; and Jenny Ruth, born March 14, 1966.

During World War II Charles went to work for the General Motors Company at the Olds Forge Plant in Lansing, Michigan, doing electrical work.

Ten years after their second son's birth, the first of three daughters, Alta May, was born on September 23, 1937. She was their little songbird, a happy child who loved to sing. An astrocytoma brain tumor took her life at age 10 on June 6, 1947.

Ruth Leone was the next daughter, born February 14, 1938. She became a registered nurse, fulfilling her Grandma Gladys' dream of a medical career for Charles. She married her high school sweetheart, Delbert G. Rinehart, on September 24, 1960. They had four children: David Charles, born May 17, 1961; Daniel Glen, born September 30, 1962; Delece Marie (Barger), born September 25, 1964; and Darrell James, born December 6, 1966. Ruth and Delbert now live in Chelan, Washington.

The third daughter of Charles and Gladys Reese was Lois Ann, born December 4, 1940. She married her high school sweetheart, Kenneth Julian, on October 8, 1961. They had two children: Rodney Kenneth, born August 3, 1965; and Corinna Rae, born February 16, 1967. Lois and Ken now live in Spokane, Washington.

In 1944 Charles moved his family from the home on Lloyd Street in Williamston to a 56-acre farm two miles east of Williamston. He farmed while also working his full-time job at the Olds Forge Plant. He retired at the age of 68 after 40 years of loyal service. He sold the farm, keeping the 5-acre hill field on which be had built a home and planted a fruit orchard (apples, pears, peaches and plums), a large strawberry patch, and a vegetable garden. They supplied fruit and vegetables for the Youth Haven Children's Camp and gave generously of what they had to those in need.

Their grandchildren loved to visit and spend time with Grandpa and Grandma Reese on the farm, where they could help with chores and fish in Grandpa's pond. Charles and Gladys lived their faith, being godly examples to their children and grandchildren. They never complained about the hardships they experienced in life but accepted them as part of God's training, choosing to become better, not bitter. What a precious legacy! Charles died June 24, 1977 at age 83, and Gladys died July 13, 1989.

(The Charles H. Reese family information was submitted by Ruth L. Rinehart and sister, Lois Ann Julian).

Harold True Reese, the youngest son of True and May Reese, was born December 8, 1904 at their West Olive home, Olive

FIGURE 25.2
True L. Reese family—1917
(back, from left) Max; Rex and wife, Grace; Robert; Earl Ellsworth, son, Sherrill, and wife, Ruth
(front, from left) True, Royal, Charles, Helen, May, and Harold

Township, Ottawa County, Michigan. On August 17, 1932 Harold married Margaret Helen Allison whom he met while attending Wheaton College, Wheaton, Illinois. She was born August 8, 1907 and died February 22, 1996 at age 88.

Harold and Margaret were the parents of three boys: James Allison, born July 2, 1934; Timothy Lee, born February 1, 1938; and John, born August 7, 1941. John died at age 20 on February 6, 1962.

There were many notable events in the life of Reverend Harold T. Reese. A life-changing event was the permanent damage caused to John by a "nasty fall" at an early age, resulting in a brain injury and a serious mental handicap. As caring parents, Harold and Margaret nurtured their son through his 20-year life at home. An occasion long remembered by many was "Harold Reese Day," November 20, 1977, in recognition of "50 Years of Faithful Service" at the First Baptist Church of Williamston, Michigan. Another was the 60th wedding anniversary of Pastor Harold and Margaret Allison Reese on August 16, 1992 (Fig. 25.3). On that day Harold preached at the Benton Street Baptist Church, Kitchener, Ontario, Canada. The message was "Marriage—Its Founding, Defending and Fulfilling." It should stand for all time as a most thoughtful and classic presentation on a subject most important in our day, or in any age.

Son James graduated from Bryan College and Grand Rapids Baptist Seminary. Jim later joined with evangelist Ken Campbell as the music partner to form "The Campbell-Reese Evangelistic Team." This experience of over 17 years led to considerable travel and gave Jim the opportunity to develop his natural musical talent. Upon leaving the team, Jim served as pastor of the Benton Street Baptist Church in Kitchener, Ontario, Canada until 2003.

Jim married Adrienne Kerr of Hammond, Indiana whom he

FIGURE 25.3
Pastor Harold and Margaret Allison Reese
celebrate their 60th wedding anniversary—August 16, 1992

had met at Bryan College. They raised a family of five children: Elizabeth, Paul, Steven, Daniel, and Philip. As young parents, Jim and Adrienne were being blessed until the birth of Steven. Several hours after Steven was born, the doctor called Jim to his office and informed him that Steven had physical abnormalities

FIGURE 25.4
Rev. James and Adrienne Reese

that would include mental retardation. This rare disorder is known as Rubinstein-Taybi Syndrome.

Adrienne recalled that both she and Jim had had experience with mentally-challenged people. Jim soon realized that of all the challenges parents face, this would not be the greatest. "Think of the sons and daughters with mental capacities, physical brawn or beauty but who are rebelling and ruining their lives," he said. "After all, Steven will have a perfect body and mind in the Hereafter!"

After looking for support groups and finding none, but

learning that their situation was not unique, Jim and Adrienne founded *Christian Horizons*. In 1976 they opened their first faith-based residential program. Over the years it has grown to serve more than 1,000 mentally- and physically-challenged children. There are now about 160 group homes in Ontario. Jim and Adrienne (Fig. 25.4) were honored as "Caring Canadians" in October 2003 by Governor-General Carkson for their many years of work helping handicapped people.

26

THE ANGELINE REESE ZEIGER FAMILY

ANGELINE Marilla Reese was born on July 5, 1862, during the early days of the Civil War. She was the fifth child and first daughter of Jacob and Sylvia House Rees, residing on the Rees farm near Wakarusa, Indiana. She grew up with younger sisters, Harmony, and Anna, attending the local country school and the First Baptist Church of Niles. There were five boys in the family:

James W., Judson W., Emory M., True L., and Hiram S.

Angeline was named after her grandmother, Angeline Mills Rees. She was about "five foot two with eyes of blue" with brown hair combed back into a bun. She always wore long dresses or skirts—which were usually black—with white pleated or patterned blouses. Often they had white lace and decorative collars. Her face was round with heavy eyelids, an inherited trait in the Rees family (17).

Being the eldest daughter in a family of mostly boys, Angeline learned at an early age to cook and help her mother. Everyone who ever ate at the table of Angeline Reese Zeiger always remembered her good country cooking

On January 8, 1884 Angeline married Daniel Zeiger. Daniel (1860–1936) grew up with his older brothers. Both of his parents had passed away by the time he was 15. By age 23 he was able to buy a farm with a house and establish himself in the farming business. The location of the farm was three miles east of Wyatt on the north side of Patterson Road in Madison Township, Indiana. Walter, Minnie, and Emory were born at this location.

FIGURE 26.1
Daniel and Angeline Zeiger

Walter, Daniel and Angeline's first child, was born

FIGURE 26.2
The Daniel Zeiger family—1894
Daniel, Walter, Minnie, Angeline, Roy (on his father's lap),
Wesley (on his mother's lap), Gertrude, and Emory

December 17, 1884 and was less than four years old when the family moved to the Chickaming Township, Michigan farm.

FIGURE 26.3
Walter J. and Alice Zeiger in 1915 with Emory and Antoinette

It was after the death of his brother, Emory, in April of 1903, that Walter, age 19, decided to get a business education and leave the farm. In September he enrolled at the South Bend Business College. He cleaned typewriters to help with his school expenses and did janitor work for his room and board. Upon receiving his diploma, he worked for the Oliver Plow Works and a year later went to work for a lumber company. In 1909, with his savings and a loan of $3,000 from his father, Walter purchased a small lumberyard in Sawyer, Michigan and started the W. J. Zeiger Lumber Company.

When the lumber and coal business was firmly established, Walter married Alice Hettelsater on October 11, 1911. They lived their entire married life in the community of Sawyer. Their first child, Emory, was born on June 16, 1912. Daughter Antoinette, was born on September 28, 1913 (Fig. 26.3).

Emory and Antoinette graduated from the St. Joseph (Michigan) High School. Walter built an attractive English style home, with a large stone fireplace, at the west end of Sawyer in the late 1920's. It was an inspiration to many. However, it was destroyed in the early 1960's when the new Interstate highway was constructed, and a truck stop was built at the Sawyer interchange.

Emory attended the University of Alabama and upon graduation with an engineering degree, was hired by his grandfather's

FIGURE 26.4
Zeiger family—1912
(*back from left*) Hiram, Roy, Wesley, Floyd Dunkelberger, Minnie, Walter
(*front from left*) Gertrude, Pearl, Angeline, Daniel, Alice, children: Erma, Emory, and Norma

company in Kansas City, Kansas, which constructed grain elevators in the midwest. Antoinette attended Northwestern University and later married Donald Helkie who had graduated from dental school and had set up a practice in South Bend, Indiana.

The second child, Minnie, born April 25, 1886, was two years old when the family moved to Michigan. At 14 she graduated from the one room Drew School, one mile west of the farm. At an early age Minnie was a great help to her mother. After Wesley was born, there were six children under the age of nine to care for.

At this time Angeline's father, Jacob, died at age 71. Her mother, Sylvia, was encouraged to move to the Zeiger farm where there was a "little house" being fixed for her. She stayed there nine years before moving back to Niles to live with her daughter, Anna.

FIGURE 26.5
Four generations—1905
Great-grandmother, Sylvia House Rees; grandmother, Angeline Reese Zeiger; mother, Minnie Dunkelberger; and daughter, Erma Dunkelberger

FIGURE 26.6
The grandchildren in 1917
(from left) Emory, Erma (holding Robert), Antoinette,
Norma (holding Vernice), and Burdette

On December 23, 1903, Minnie married Floyd Dunkelberger of Three Oaks, Michigan, and they set up housekeeping in the "little house." Floyd was a man of many talents, working in the local creamery and on the farm. Their first child, Erma, was born December 22, 1904 (See Fig. 26.5). Norma was born June 11, 1907. The family moved to Three Oaks when Floyd began working at the creamery in town. After World War I they moved to Dowagiac, Michigan where there was a need for employees for the home heating furnace factories. A third daughter, Mona, was born September 1, 1917 (17).

Emory was born February 11, 1888, six months prior to the

move to the farm in Michigan. Emory was not a strong child and died at age 15 on April 11, 1903. Medical information available in later years would indicate he died from what is now known as juvenile diabetes.

The first child born at the farm was Gertrude, on September 11, 1889. She was 13 at the time her Grandmother Rees moved to Niles to live with daughter Anna Andrews, and 14 when her sister, Minnie, was married. Gertrude attended high school in Three Oaks. Her attention to and help with her younger brother, Hiram, and niece, Erma, served to influence her to become a teacher of young children.

Gertrude finished high school in June 1908 with a class of 12 and took a county examination allowing her to teach grade school.

She filled a vacancy at the local Drew School and taught there for three years. In the fall of 1911 she enrolled in Western State Normal in Kalamazoo to obtain a permanent teaching

FIGURE 26.7
Gertrude as primary grades teacher at Riverside School, 1908–09

certificate. Following her graduation in 1913, Gertrude accepted a teaching position in White Pigeon, Michigan. After a year at White Pigeon she accepted a position in the Elkhart, Indiana schools.

At home during the summer of 1913, she met a new neighbor. Arthur Johnson, from Chicago, was spending the summer with his mother and sister. The John Johnson family had purchased the farm where the True Reese family had lived from 1888 to 1902. Upon learning she could leave her Elkhart position in March, she took the train to Chicago to be married. Arthur had arranged with his Uncle Nils and Aunt Hilda Hassel to be married in their home on March 11, 1915.

FIGURE 26.8
Gertrude graduates from Western State in 1913.

Arthur and Gertrude set up housekeeping in an apartment on Grand Boulevard in Chicago. Arthur had completed a course at Bryan Strattan Business College and was employed with Swift and Company, a large meat packing company near the stockyards in Chicago. Their first child, Robert, was born June 23, 1916 at St. Luke's Hospital in Chicago.

With the United States entry in World War I on April 6,

1917, obligations and opportunities caused many to rethink their future. The young Johnson family moved back to Michigan where Arthur began work at Clark Equipment Company in Buchanan. It was at this location that two more sons were born: John, on January 9, 1918, and Walter, on August 11, 1919.

By 1920, when the war production effort had declined and the price of food was on the rise, it seemed to be a good time to move to the John Johnson farm. The place was vacant except for a few summer months when Arthur's mother liked to leave the city. Indoor plumbing had been installed and water was available from a deep well. Although Arthur was not raised to be a farmer, he had the ability and energy as well as a likeness for outdoor

FIGURE 26.9
Arthur and Gertrude Johnson with sons Walter, John, and Robert

life. The barn was enlarged to accommodate a six- to eight-cow dairy herd, and a grain storage facility was built. A daughter, Ruth, was born at this location on December 1, 1920.

In 1926 Arthur's father announced his retirement and expected to live on the farm. Arthur and Gertrude purchased the Roy Zeiger 80 acres, bordering on the west. There were no buildings on the property. The family moved in with Daniel Zeiger, who was now living alone since Angeline had died, until a house could be built on the 80 acres. A fourth son, Reese, was born on July 22, 1926, at this rather difficult time. The new house was finished in August 1927 so the family could move into it.

It was with these bare essentials that the five children started a new and settled life and grew to maturity. They all attended the local 8-grade school, now named The Riverside School, and went on to Three Oaks High School.

Robert and John went on to graduate from Michigan State University; Robert in Chemical Engineering and John (J. D.) in Agriculture Extension Service. He first taught at the high school level, then became County Agricultural Agent in Berrien County and later in Eaton County.

Robert was employed in Los Angeles, California and Jackson, Michigan with public utility engineering and research laboratories. Robert also completed R.O.T.C. training at Michigan State and spent five years, less two months, in active military service in World War II, serving in North Africa and Italy with a unit of the Fifth Army Artillery.

Walter graduated as salutatorian of his high school class and went on to the University of Michigan where he received a degree in Architecture. The City of Detroit then employed him in city planning, and at the same time, he attended Wayne State University to obtain a L.L.B. degree in law. Walter was subsequently employed as City Planner for Madison, Wisconsin. At that time he attended the University of Wisconsin where he earned a J.D. Doctorate of Law.

Upon graduating from high school in 1939, Ruth attended Michigan State for a year. By 1941 she was employed in an essential war production company in Jackson, Michigan.

Reese left Three Oaks High School after his junior year, transferring to Bob Jones Academy in Cleveland, Tennessee where he obtained his high school diploma in 1945. He then went on to Bob Jones University where he received his Bachelor of Arts degree. He next attended Grace Seminary at Winona Lake, Indiana where he earned a Master of Divinity degree (cum laude). He served as pastor of Baptist churches in Indiana and Illinois.

Arthur and Gertrude sold the farm to Gertrude's brother, Wesley, in 1955 and had a home built in Harbert for their retirement. Arthur continued to work into his later years doing landscape work with Seeders and on his own.

Gertrude had a heart attack in October 1955, the same month that then President Eisenhower had a cardiac infraction. Although at a much slower pace, she lived another ten years to enjoy her family. Gertrude passed away in August 1965, a month before her 76th birthday. Arthur enjoyed an active life until he broke his hip in 1982. He died in February 1984 after some months in a nursing home.

Roy (Fig. 26.10), the third son of Daniel and Angeline Zieger, was born on the farm on October 26, 1891. Roy was an energetic boy, adapting well to the work on the farm. He completed his schooling at the Drew School and on March 12, 1912 married Pearl Brant (Fig. 26.11). They set up housekeeping in the "little house" on the farm. To Roy's credit, his adventure in farming was a great success. He raised wheat on his land during some of the World War I years when the demand was great and the price, high.

A daughter, Burdette, was born April 30, 1914. Always the attractive, cheerful little girl, Burdette became quite popular. She attended the New Troy School and completed high school at St. Mary's Academy, South Bend, Indiana. The family left the farm in May of 1920, moving to Sawyer where Roy joined his brother Walter in the Zeiger Lumber Company as a partner.

One spring in the late 1930's, Burdette was chosen to be "Miss Sawyer", representing the town in the Blossomland Festival and Parade held in May each year (Fig. 26.12).

The Lumber Company prospered as lakeshore and adjacent property values increased and building hit a boom time. Roy had a home built to his specifications in Shorewood Hills, named "Dream Castle." On March 11, 1959 Roy suffered a heart

FIGURE 26.10
Roy Zeiger (about 1907)

FIGURE 26.11
Pearl Brant Zeiger (about 1965)

Miss Burdette Zeiger, brunette, was cheered by an overflow crowd at the Flynn theatre last night when she was chosen "Miss Sawyer" in the Blossom festival.

FIGURE 26.12
"Miss Sawyer," Burdette Zeiger, 1935 Blossamland Festival

attack and passed away at age 67. In July following this sad event, the Zeiger family started a series of annual reunions that lasted for over 25 years. Pearl spent her winters in St. Petersburg, Florida and passed away in 1977 at 87 years of age.

On September 13, 1893, a fourth son, Wesley, was born to Daniel and Angeline. It was at this time that Angeline's health seemed to decline. It was also noted that Emory was not as strong and sturdy as the other children. The "little house" was remodeled for Grandmother Rees who offered to come and help with the six children.

Wesley finished the eighth grade at the Drew School and attended Three Oaks High School for over a year. He enjoyed the farm activities, which seemed more important to him than high school. On January 31, 1916 he married Dagmar Jensen and they began housekeeping in the Johnson house, just to the west of the farm. Four years later when Roy's family moved to Sawyer, Wesley's family moved into the "little house," now consisting of Vernice, born July 15, 1916 and Kathryn, born November 2, 1918.

FIGURE 26.13
The Wesley Zeiger family—1919
Dagmar, Katherine, Vernice, and Wesley

Farming came naturally to Wesley. Those who knew him believed the remark said of him: "he thrived on work." Thelma was born October 3, 1922 and Wesley, Jr. was born August 11, 1926. By the next fall Wesley took over total responsibility for the operation of the farm. In the summer of 1920 the house had been remodeled to accommodate two families. After Hiram left the farm, Wesley and family moved into the east side of the house.

Vernice graduated from Three Oaks High School in 1934 and from the County Normal in 1936 with a teaching certificate. She taught school in the Spring Creek School south of Three Oaks and the Bell School in Cass County. Vernice married Joseph Beck in 1941 and died in childbirth on February 17, 1943.

Kathryn graduated from Three Oaks High School in 1940. Wesley, Jr. left school in 1944, joined the army, and served with the occupying forces in Europe.

Hiram, the seventh child of Angeline and Daniel, was born October 19, 1898 at the time of the Spanish American War. Grandmother Rees left after Hiram was four and the older children were more help. She moved to Niles to live with her youngest daughter, Anna, and her husband, Wesley Andrews, and to attend her home church, the First Baptist Church of Niles (Fig. 23.1).

Hiram was known to be a jovial person, often very helpful as well as sometimes mischievous. In the middle of a most severe winter, January 1918, he obtained a sled load of coal and with a team of horses, brought it to the Johnson home in Buchanan. Hiram was also the first of the boys on the Zeiger farm to have an automobile of his own—a Model T Ford.

FIGURE 26.14
Hiram and Lillian Zeiger—1920 wedding photo

On the 29th of September 1920, Hiram married Lillian Morton in LaPorte, Indiana. The Mortons, a family of four girls, lived near Rolling Prairie, south and east of Three Oaks, just across the state line. Hiram and Lillian began their married life on the farm, living in the eastern half of the remodeled house of his parents.

During the years on the farm, Hiram and Lillian

became the parents of three boys. Roy, born July 7, 1921, was the first grandson born on the farm. Sometime after graduating from Three Oaks High School, Roy volunteered for military service. His first training assignment was at Fort Sill, Oklahoma with the field artillery. When the Army Air Corp. was looking for young men for pilot training, Roy responded and took his training at the air base near San Antonio, Texas. In 1943 he was assigned to the 5th Air Force flying bombing runs from a North African base to the Polesti Oil Fields in Romania. It was on a mission, flying a B-24 bomber, that he was shot down, losing his life with the crew, as happened with many flights to the Romanian Oil Fields.

On June 21, 1923 Rex was born to Hiram and Lillian. He graduated from Three Oaks High School in 1941. His business venture in the Salt Lake City area involved the acquisition, treatment, and sale of large timbers, including the operation of a wood preservative treatment plant.

Harold, the third son of Hiram and Lillian, was born July 7, 1925. After high school, Harold joined the Army, serving with armored units at Fort Knox and overseas in Europe during the latter part of World War II. In the fall of 1926, Hiram moved his family to Sawyer where he took over the hardware part of the Zieger Lumber and Coal Company. A daughter, Elinor, was born in Sawyer on August 29, 1927. She graduated from Three Oaks High School in 1945.

Hiram and Lillian retired to a location on Red Bud Trail, north of Buchanan and spent the winter months at their home in Winter Haven, Florida. Lillian died in her sleep in their Florida home on April 30, 1971. Some time later, Hiram moved back to Michigan and passed away on March 12, 1976.

Our beloved Grandmother, Angeline Reese Zeiger, passed away on October 3, 1924 following a gall bladder operation at

St. Anthony Hospital in Michigan City, Indiana. The obituary in the *Three Oaks Acorn* read,

> Mrs. Zeiger was quiet, unassuming in manner, kind and sympathetic in all her ways, somewhat like the excellent woman described in the Bible, Proverbs 31:10–28. She was held in high esteem by relatives and neighbors as was evidenced by the large number in attendance at her funeral.

The casket was open at home for a time and a black wreath was placed on the west door, as was the custom at that time. Many of her 19 grandchildren were brought to see their grandmother for the last time.

Although the farm was operated by Wesley, Grandfather Zeiger continued to be of help. In the 1920's he owned a Buick sedan with side curtains, followed by a Studebaker four-door around 1930. After he bought a Dodge automobile in 1934, he felt comfortable driving to Florida for a few winter months. His grandson Emory helped with driving on occasion.

Grandfather Zeiger passed away on April 16, 1936 at the St. Joseph Sanatorium due to pneumonia following surgery. His death brought great sorrow to the family and condolences from many in the township with whom he had served at various times as supervisor and treasurer. Many details in the lives of Angeline Reese and Daniel Zeiger (Fig. 26.15) are noted in *The Zeiger Centennial Farm,* published in 1988 (17).

FIGURE 26.15
Daniel and Angeline Reese Zeiger—1912

27

THE ANN ADELLE REESE HUNTLY FAMILY

ANN (ANNIE) Adelle Reese was born May 21, 1850 at the Barron Lake residence, Howard Township, Cass County, Michigan home of Judson Wade Rees. She was the only daughter of Judson Wade, who at nine years of age, came to Michigan with his parents, John Melancthon and Angeline Mills Rees. Ann Adelle's mother was Catherine Maria Willard, born June 15, 1825 in Herkimer County, New York.

On September 29, 1879 Annie married George Gordon Huntly, the son of Ephraim and Eliza Ross Huntly.

Annie and Gordon's children were Eugene Reese, Winfred Wade, Mary Louise, and Clarence Gordon.

Judd Reese, the brother of Annie, was born July 17, 1852. He married Phoebe Ellen Green on September 5, 1876. There were no children from this union.

Eugene Reese was born on July 6, 1880 also at the Barron Lake farm home and died there on September 20, 1954. Eugene married Grace Elizabeth Doane on June 27, 1906. "Gene" was the congenial host of the Reese reunions at the old Victorian style home of Barron Lake (Figs. 20.1–20.4).

The children of Eugene and Grace were Dorothy Jeanne, born May 26, 1906, married to Frederick Taylor; and Mary Elaine, born December 17, 1908, married to John F. Bowen. Dorothy and Frederick had two children and nine grandchildren. Elaine and John had two children and six grandchildren.

Winfred Wade was born at the Barron Lake home on October 5, 1882 and died in Roswell, New Mexico on April 23, 1962. He married Kotzie Willard on December 25, 1905. Their children were Gordon, who died as an infant in 1906; Murial Louise, born November 10, 1907, married to George Zimmerman; Catherine Ann, born March 10, 1909; and George Eugene, born June 30, 1912 in Niles, Michigan. George married Helen Jane Willard. There were seven grandchildren.

The third child of Ann Adelle and Gordon was Mary Louise, born April 10, 1884 at the Barron Lake home. "Louise" married Leo Arthur Skinner who was born on September 13, 1879. They lived and died in the Detroit area, having one son and five grandchildren.

The fourth child, Clarence Gordon, was born January 27, 1887. He married Gladys Eggleston. They had a daughter, Mary Elizabeth, who married another George Gordon Huntly and gave Gordon and Gladys a granddaughter.

Dorothy Jeanne, best remembered as Dorothy Taylor, studied materials her father received in 1942 from Ivy Huntley Horn of Herndon, Virginia, in an effort to understand or verify the family's genealogy. The Huntly name has sometimes been spelled with an "e."

In 1982 Dorothy visited Scotland and spent some time in the town of Huntly, including a visit to the Huntly Castle. The town is in the Grampians on the River Deveron, northwest of Aberdeen and south of Banff. The names of the 4th, 5th, 6th, and 7th Earl of Huntly and the names of the 1st and 2nd Marquis of Huntly were George Gordon Huntly. The town and castle are in an area of the Clan Gordon.

Information on the Huntly family has been made available by Edwin Willard of Niles, Michigan.

Cymru—"Land of Fellow Countrymen"

The identifying icon for the final section, *Part VII—Epilogue,* is the Welsh flag featuring the national emblem bright red dragon on white and green background panels.

PART VII
Epilogue

28
WALES TODAY

WHEN we turn our attention to Wales today, it may be easy to say, "It's no different than any other modern English speaking land." There are some shopping malls with nice stores and quality things to buy. There are stadiums for great athletic events. There are beaches and resorts for grand vacations. However, beyond all this there are some of the world's great music and poetry festivals that attract large numbers of people. There are many castles and historical sites that attract the artist, the history buff, and the academician. The list goes on and on.

Also, there is a deeper meaning to much of what is seen in Wales today. A considerable number of people interested in their ancestral homeland come to Wales. The University of Wales,

University of Wales, Aberystwyth

Library and Museum is in the west coast city of Aberystwyth. The quest for family records is not so different than the quest for Camelot.

Known as *The Lyric Land,* Wales is the country of bards and saints where great castles anchor the present to the past and the legend of *King Arthur and the Knights of the Round Table.* More than most nations on earth, Wales lives in spirit if not in fact. It is also the land of Christian saints such as Dewi Sant, Patrick, Christmas Evans, and many others.

Dewi Sant

Modern factories now rise in the place of mining and molten metal works. The director of the famed Pendyrus Male Choir has stated, "It's factory hands and office workers now. But they can still sing. We have not been wealthy people, but we have our voice."

Chapter 28—Wales Today   289

City Centre, Swansea

Mr. Neil Rees, the professional City Manager of Swansea, is the chief strategist of a vigorous plan to develop the city's 900-acre waterfront with new factories, indoor playing fields, a swimming pool, etc. The visitor

Cardiff Castle, Cardiff

getting off the train in Carmarthen, will see a large sign: "REES SOUND" with a phone number. Such signs are unusual. In Cardiff, the Angel Hotel is a fine location close to Queens Street shopping, across the street from Cardiff Castle grounds and a short walk to the railway station.

In the rolling hills just north of Beacons National Park is the quaint little medieval market town of Hay on Wye, known for its many second-hand book shops. It is a fascinating place where

Hay on Wye

all sense of time is lost.

Running north and south in the center of Wales are the Cambrian Mountains. This area in the center of Wales is almost unknown except by old shepherds and farmers. Sheep graze freely and in great numbers throughout a good part of Wales. Some have said the country has more sheep than people.

Wales is, however, a land where nature prevails in its marvelous wilderness, lonely and boggy. Wynford Vaughan-Thomas, a TV commentator and guide, has said, "Much of our poetry springs from our love of nature. It may be the secret of the Welsh soul.

Cambrian Mountains, central Wales

Our greatest medieval poet, Dafydd ap Gwilym, was a lyric genius in Chaucer's time. He wrote in a complex system called *cynghanedd,* which requires precise ordering of consonants, alliteration, internal rhyme, and a sonance of special places. It is disciplined music, and with thought and emotion, it can be terrifyingly powerful." Some of the world's greatest poetic utterances are found in Welsh. Although the feeling may come through, much effect may be lost in translation.

Dylan Thomas (1914–1953)

Although few might understand these great utterances in Welsh, Dylan Thomas of the last century, spoke no Welsh but grew up in an atmosphere of Welsh eloquence. Drink was his undoing. Away from his homeland he knew and responded to bardic discipline. Before his death at

Cardiff, capital city of Wales

Emblematic daffodils adorn Wales

age 39, he recorded, "Death shall have no dominion," his voice rising, rising, harking back to the chants of the bards, rhythmic, spellbinding, called the *hwyl*. The old Methodist preachers were masters of it, and could move whole chapels to ecstasy.

So, there are echoes of yesterday in the Wales of today. One Welsh farmer calls his sheep "antelopes in wooly pullovers" (right).

The willful and nonconformist sheep range freely through the hill country. They are fitting symbols of a country whose sense of independence has never been diminished (42).

As castles guarded the way in times past
There is now peace in the valleys at last.

Bibliography

1. *The Reformation & Protestantism,* Indianapolis, 2002 by James S. Bell, Jr. & Tracy M. Sumner, 385 pages
2. *The Illustrated History of Britain,* New York, 1979, by A. L. Rowse, 185 pages
3. *A History of Wales,* London, 1993 by John Davies, 718 pages
4. *Wales* (A Travel Guidebook), London, 2001 by John King, 336 pages
5. *Famous Welsh Battles,* New York, 1977 by Philip Warner, 160 pages
6. *The Xenophobe's Guide to the Welsh,* London, 1994 by John Winterson Richards, 64 pages
7. *The Medieval Lordship of Brecon,* Cardiff, 1968 by William Rees (Brecon Society), 106 pages

8. *Wales (An Inspired View),* London 1966 by R. M. Lockley, 207 pages

9. *West Stockbridge Massachusetts,* Great Barrington, 1974 by Edna Bailey Garnet, 136 pages

10. *A Matter of Wales,* Oxford, 1984 by Jan Morris, 450 pages

11. *Horizon,* Vol. L, New York, 1958

12. *Modern Wales* (c. 1485–1979), Cambridge, 1984 by Gareth Elwyn Jones, 365 pages

13. *Heraldry,* New York, 1970 by Ottfried & Neubecker

14. *The Wars of the Roses* by Desmond Seward

15. *How the Irish Saved Civilization,* 1995 by Thomas Cahill, 250 pages

16. *Treasury of Name Lore,* Evanston, 1967 by Edson C. Smith, 246 pages

17. *Family Names,* New York, 1982 by J. N. Hook, Ph.D., 388 pages

18. *In the Lions Court,* London, 2002 by Derek Wilson, 592 pages

19. *The Welsh People,* New York and London, 1924 by Sir John Rhys & Sir David Jones, 670 pages

20. *Studies in Welsh History,* Cardiff, 1947 by J.F. Rees, 175 pages

21. *South Wales and the March 1284–1415,* London, 1924 by W. Rees

22. *Celtic Heritage,* London by Alwyn & Brinley Rees

Bibliography 297

23. *The Holy Bible* (King James Version)
24. *King Henry VIII—A Pitkin Guide,* Norwich, 1999 by Angela Roystri, 24 pages
25. *Warrior Kings and Princes of Britain 1066–1422,* Pilgrim Press, 1995 by Robert C. Carnegie, 24 pages
26. *Her Majesty's Tower of London—A Pitkin Guide,* Andover, 1991 by Olwen Hedley, 20 pages
27. *The Wars of the Roses—Osprey History,* 1983 by Terrence Wise, 40 pages
28. *Celtic Wales—A Pitkin Guide,* Andover, 1997 by John Watney, 28 pages
29. *The Ultimate Guide to Christian History,* Uhrichsville, 2001 by Carol and Roddy Smith, 435 pages
30. *Exploring the World of King Arthur,* London, 2000 by Christopher Snyder, 190 pages
31. *The Tudors in Britain,* London, 1999 by Richard Wood, 32 pages
32. *The Last Welsh Prince of Wales Military History,* 2002 by John Latimer
33. *King Edward's Conquest of Wales Military History,* 1999 by Paul V. Walsh
34. *Royal Map of Great Britain,* Edinburgh by L. P. G. Dow of Bartholomew & Sons, Ltd.
35. *Chieftains and Princes* (Welsh), Cardiff, 1996 by Charles Kightly, 36 pages
36. *Over Wales—A Pitkin Unichrome,* Andover, 2000 by Vivien Brett, 32 pages

37. *Dungeons & Torture—A Pitkin Guide,* Andover, 1998 by John McIlwain, 24 pages

38. *Castles of Wales—A Pitkin Guide,* Andover, 2001 by David Cook & Vivien Brett, 30 pages

39. *Welsh Castles,* Ceredigion, 2001 by Geraint Roberts, 72 pages

40. *Celtic Mysticism,* London, 2000 by Anthony Duncan, 64 pages

41. *Britain and Ireland,* Washington D.C., 1985 National Geographic Society

42. *Wales, The Lyric Land,* Washington D.C. 1983 by Bryan Hodgson, National Geographic Society

43. *Who Really Was St. Patrick?—A Sermon* by Dr. D. James Kennedy

44. *The Rees/Race Family in America,* 1987 by John R. Powers & W. B. Race

45. *The Name and Family of Rees(e),* New York, 1984 by Roots Research Bureau, Ltd., 11 pages

46. *A Rare Bit of Walsh,* Ft. Lauderdale, 1993 by Pamela Petro (*Sun-Sentinel* 3/14)

47. *In Search of Saint David,* 1992 by Paul Moorcraft

48. *The England and Holland of the Pilgrims,* London, 1906 by Henry M. and Morton Dexter, 670 pages

49. *Carmarthenshire—Garden of Wales and Town Guide* Carmarthen, 2000, 49 pages

50. *Heritage Wales,* Cardiff, 2002, 50 pages

51. *Annals and Antiquities of the County and County Families of Wales* (2 vols.), London, 1872 by Thomas Nicholas, 948 pages

52. *The Green Guide—Wales,* France, 2001 by Michelin Travel Publications, 326 pages

53. *St. Peters Parish Church,* Carmarthen, 1997, Notes for Visitors, 6 pages

54. *King Arthur's Labyrinth,* Bards Quest, 2002

55. *The Reformers—Calvin & Zwingli,* Leicester, 1972 by John Broome, B.A., 24 pages

56. *Life in a Medieval Castle,* New York, 1974 by Joseph and Frances Gies, 272 pages

57. *Wales Castles and Historic Places,* London, 1990 by D. M. Robinson and R. S. Thomas, 135 pages

58. *Encyclopedia Britannica,* Vols. 9 & 11, London, 1958

59. *The Gillett Families in America,* Fondulac, 1953 by Esther Gillett Latham

60. *Biographical Notes to R. L. Johnson,* 1980 by Ruth Reese Bigsby

61. *The John and Mary—1630,* Vol. 2, 1935 (a search for passengers)

62. *Kingdom of the Celts—A History and Guide,* London, 1998 by John King, 256 pages

63. *Genealogies and Biographies of Ancient Windsor,* Connecticut

64. *The World and Its Peoples,* New York, 1966, Greystone Press

65. *The Discovery of King Arthur,* New York, 1985, by Geoffrey Ashe, 224 pages

Photo credits for chapter 28, *Wales Today*

University of Wales, Aberystwyth (p. 288)
http://www.bbc.co.uk/wales/mid/fun/wallpaper/pages/images/aber_old_college1024.jpg

Dewi Sant (p. 288)
www.smo.uhi.ac.uk/~sm99dp00/cuimris/dewi-sant.jpg

City Centre, Swansea (p. 289)
http://www.public.iastate.edu/~acjohn55/PhotoGalleries/CityOfSwansea/images/SANY0506.JPG

Cardiff Castle, Cardiff (p. 289)
Roger C. Bowen, in *A Jarrold Guide to the Welsh Capital City of Cardiff*

Hay on Wye (p. 290)
http://www.jswebsite.co.uk/img-html/wales-hay-on-wye-mar-2003-1/20030406-031039.htm

Cambrian Mountains, central Wales (p. 290)
http://www.bbc.co.uk/wales/mid/fun/wallpaper/pages/images/cambrian_mts_foel_fadian1152.jpg

Swansea City Opera logo (p. 291)
http://www.btinternet.com/~llantilio/scologo.jpg

Dylan Thomas (p. 291)
www.poetryconnection.net/images/Dylan_Thomas.jpg

Cardiff, capital city of Wales (p. 291)
http://www.neth.de/Pics/Wales/Cardiff/Cardiff_SouthWest_M.jpg

Emblematic daffodils adorn Wales (p. 292)
http://www.jswebsite.co.uk/img-html/wales-hay-on-wye-mar-2003-1/20030406-054259.htm

Photo (p. 293) courtesy of The National Geographic Society